PRE-CALCULUS
ANSWER KEY & TEST BANK

Table of Contents

Problem Set Answers ———————————————— 1

Chapter Tests ———————————————— 45

Chapter Tests Answers ———————————————— 99

Pre-Calculus: A Teaching Textbook™
2.0 Version
Answer Key and Test Bank
Greg Sabouri

Printed in the United States of America.

ISBN: 978-0-9835812-9-1

Teaching Textbooks, Inc.
6710 N. Classen Blvd.
Oklahoma City, OK 73116
www.teachingtextbooks.com

find the
answers
graphically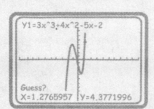

factory costs are
a linear function

PROBLEM SET ANSWERS

$\left|\begin{matrix} a & b \\ c & d \end{matrix}\right| = ad - bc \;\; \}value$

just cross multiply and
then subtract

$\cos 2u = \begin{cases} \cos^2 u - \sin^2 u \\ 2\cos^2 u - 1 \\ 1 - 2\sin^2 u \end{cases}$

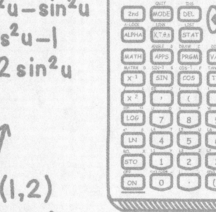

exponential
functions

$y = 2^x$

$(-1, 2)$ $(1, 2)$

$(0, 1)$

$y = \left(\frac{1}{2}\right)^x$ or 2^{-x}

reflects across

$x^3 + 2x^2 - 5x - 6 = 0$

$(x-2)(x+3)(x+1) = 0$

CHAPTER 1

Practice 1
a. $y = -14$
b. Yes
c. Yes
d. No
e. B

Problem Set 1
1. True
2. True
3. False
4. $y = 14$
5. $y = 0$
6. $y = 1$
7. $y = -1$
8. No
9. Yes
10. No
11. Yes
12. C
13. B
14. D
15. A
16. Yes
17. No
18. Yes
19. No
20. E
21. D
22. B

Practice 2
a. Independent variable: t;
   Dependent variable: y
b. $f(-3) = 41$
c. C
d. $x = 33$
e. C

Problem Set 2
1. False
2. False
3. C
4. D
5. Yes
6. No
7. No
8. Yes
9. Yes

10. A
11. C
12. Independent variable: s;
    Dependent variable: q
13. Independent variable: k;
    Dependent variable: l
14. $f(4) = 5$
15. $f(-2) = 11$
16. C
17. B
18. $x = -2$
19. $x = 26$
20. E
21. A
22. D

Practice 3
a. B
b. D
c. A
d. E
e. C

Problem Set 3
1. True
2. True
3. $y = 5$
4. $y = -9$
5. No
6. Yes
7. B
8. C
9. D
10. -9
11. -19
12. B
13. D
14. A
15. E
16. $x = 9$
17. $x = -\dfrac{3}{8}$
18. E
19. B
20. A
21. C
22. D

Practice 4

a. A

b. y = r(x)

x	3	-1	0	2	-3	-4	1
y	-27	-3	0	-12	-27	-48	-3

y = k(x)

x	-3 (or 3)	1 (or -1)	0	-2	3 (or -3)	4	-1 (or 1)
y	-27	-3	0	-12	-27	-48	-3

c. B

d. B

e. C

Problem Set 4

1. True
2. False
3. Yes
4. No
5. B
6. A
7. $x = -3$
8. $x = -2$
9. D
10. E
11. B
12. A
13. C
14. B
15. B
16. D
17. y = f(x)

x	-2	-1	0	1	2	3	4
y	-12	-3	0	3	-12	-27	-48

y = g(x)

x	-2	-1	0	1	2	3	4
y	12	3	0	-3	12	27	48

18. y = h(x)

x	4	1	0	-2	-1	-3	2
y	128	2	0	-16	-2	-54	16

y = p(x)

x	-4	-1	0	2	1	3	-2
y	128	2	0	-16	-2	-54	16

19. C
20. C

21. A
22. B

Practice 5

a. A

b. B

c. C

d. y = k(x)

x	-10	-6	-2	0	4	8
y	119	49	11	4	14	56

e. A

Problem Set 5

1. True
2. True
3. D
4. C
5. A
6. E
7. A
8. E
9. E
10. A
11. B
12. C
13. A
14. D
15. A
16. C
17. y = g(x)

x	-4	-1	0	2	3	4
y	144	27	12	18	39	72

18. y = r(x)

x	-8	-2	0	4	6	8
y	48	9	4	6	13	24

19. y = h(x)

x	-4	-1	0	2	3	4
y	12	2.25	1	1.5	3.25	6

20. y = p(x)

x	-2	-0.5	0	1	1.5	2
y	48	9	4	6	13	24

21. D
22. A

Practice 6

a. A
b. $f(x(1)) = 3$
c. D
d. B
e. E

Problem Set 6

1. True
2. True
3. B
4. C
5. y = b(x)

x	-1	-0.5	-0.25	0	1	2
y	16	12		10	8	0	-8

6. y = c(x)

x	-4	-2	-1	0	4	8
y	8	6	5	4	0	-4

7. y = d(x)

x	-16	-8	-4	0	16	32
y	16	12	10	8	0	-8

8. B
9. E
10. C
11. D
12. E
13. $f(x(2)) = 3$
14. $f(x(-1)) = 2$
15. $f(x(1)) = 4$
16. E
17. A
18. E
19. D
20. C
21. B
22. E

Practice 7

a. E
b. C
c. C
d. B
e. D

Problem Set 7

1. True
2. True

3. True
4. D
5. E
6. A
7. C
8. A
9. E
10. B
11. D
12. $f(x(1)) = 2$
13. $f(x(6)) = 5$
14. E
15. D
16. C
17. A
18. E
19. C
20. A
21. D
22. A

CHAPTER 2

Practice 8
a. Slope $= 0$; y-intercept: $(0,7)$
b. B
c. Slope $= -\dfrac{1}{4}$
d. C
e. D
f. 15 batteries

Problem Set 8
1. True
2. False
3. Slope $= 5$; y-intercept: $(0, -3)$
4. Slope $= -2$; y-intercept: $(0,7)$
5. Slope $= 0$; y-intercept: $(0, -5)$
6. A
7. C
8. Slope $= 5$
9. Slope $= \dfrac{3}{4}$
10. C
11. A
12. E
13. B
14. B
15. B
16. D
17. $f(x(-2)) = 12$
18. $f(x(4)) = 21$
19. C
20. E
21. E
22. B
23. 24 donuts

Practice 9
a. Slope $= -\dfrac{5}{6}$; y-intercept: $(0,6)$
b. A
c. D
d. x-intercepts: $(1,0)$ and $(-1.25,0)$; y-intercept: $(0, -5)$
e. x-intercepts: $(0.68,0)$ and $(-0.88,0)$
f. 0.25 seconds

Problem Set 9
1. True
2. True

3. False
4. Slope $= -\dfrac{3}{2}$; y-intercept: $(0,3)$
5. Slope $= 0$; y-intercept: $(0,8)$
6. D
7. C
8. Slope $= -\dfrac{5}{2}$
9. Slope $= 3$
10. D
11. B
12. $y = p(x)$

x	-1	-0.4	-0.2	0	0.6	1.4
y	24	18	9	-2	-7	-10

13. $y = q(x)$

x	-5	-2	-1	0	3	7
y	8	6	3	-0.7	-2.3	-3.3

14. E
15. C
16. D
17. A
18. x-intercepts: $(0,0)$ and $(-2,0)$; y-intercept: $(0,0)$
19. x-intercepts: $(3,0)$ and $(2,0)$; y-intercept: $(0,6)$
20. x-intercepts: $(2,0)$ and $(-0.5,0)$; y-intercept: $(0, -2)$
21. x-intercepts: $(0.88,0)$ and $(-1.88,0)$
22. x-intercepts: $(1.19,0)$ and $(-1.69,0)$
23. 6.25 seconds

Practice 10
a. Slope $= \dfrac{1}{3}$; y-intercept: $(0, -\dfrac{5}{3})$
b. Vertex: $(2, -9)$
c. D
d. A
e. B
f. 20 feet

Problem Set 10
1. True
2. False
3. Slope $= -4$; y-intercept: $(0,1)$
4. Slope $= \dfrac{1}{5}$; y-intercept: $(0, -\dfrac{3}{4})$

5. Slope $= \dfrac{1}{2}$; y-intercept: $(0, \dfrac{3}{2})$

6. B

7. A

8. x-intercepts: $(0,0)$ and $(\dfrac{1}{2},0)$

   y-intercept: $(0,0)$

9. x-intercepts: $(2,0)$ and $(\dfrac{3}{2},0)$

   y-intercept: $(0,6)$

10. x-intercepts: $(0.72,0)$ and $(-1.39,0)$

11. x-intercepts: $(2.35,0)$ and $(-0.85,0)$

12. Vertex: $(-1,-3)$

13. Vertex: $(2,4)$

14. Vertex: $(3,-16)$

15. C

16. A

17. E

18. B

19. D

20. E

21. D

22. B

23. 8 feet

8. $f(x) = \dfrac{1}{2}x^5$

x	-2	-1	0	1	2
y	-16	-0.5	0	0.5	16

9. $g(x) = -3x^5$

x	-2	-1	0	1	2
y	96	3	0	-3	-96

10. C

11. A

12. Vertex: $(5,8)$

13. Vertex: $(-2,-7)$

14. B

15. A

16. E

17. C

18. D

19. B

20. D

21. B

22. E

23. 20 feet

Practice 11

a. No

b. $g(x) = -4x^5$

x	-2	-1	0	1	2
y	128	4	0	-4	-128

c. E

d. A

e. C

f. 80 feet

Problem Set 11

1. True

2. True

3. Yes

4. No

5. No

6. $f(x) = 3x^4$

x	-2	-1	0	1	2
y	48	3	0	3	48

7. $g(x) = -2x^4$

x	-2	-1	0	1	2
y	-32	-2	0	-2	-32

Practice 12

a. C

b. B

c. No

d. 3 turning points

e. C

f. 1.5 seconds

Problem Set 12

1. True

2. True

3. E

4. D

5. $g(f(2)) + f(1) = 5$

6. D

7. $f(x) = -3x^3 + 4x + 2$

x	-3	-2	0	2	3
y	71	18	2	-14	-67

8. $g(x) = 2x^4 - x^3 + 7x^2$

x	-3	-2	0	2	3
y	252	68	0	52	198

9. Vertex: $(-3,-1)$

10. Vertex: $\left(\dfrac{3}{4},3\right)$

11. C
12. E
13. A
14. B
15. D
16. C
17. Yes
18. No
19. No
20. 2 turning points
21. 3 turning points
22. D
23. A
24. A
25. 2.5 seconds

Practice 13
a. D
b. D
c. Remainder = 126
d. C
e. Zeros: -1, 1, 2
f. 6 seconds

Problem Set 13
1. True
2. True
3. False
4. B
5. E
6. No
7. Yes
8. 2 turning points
9. 3 turning points
10. B
11. C
12. C
13. B
14. D
15. No
16. Yes
17. No
18. Remainder = 8
19. Remainder = -28
20. A
21. E
22. Zeros: -2, 0, 3
23. Zeros: -4, 1, 2
24. Zeros: -1, 1, 2
25. 5 seconds

Practice 14
a. B
b. D
c. 7th degree
d. Zeros: -3, $-\sqrt{3}$, $\sqrt{3}$
e. C
f. 3 minutes; 12 minutes

Problem Set 14
1. True
2. False
3. Slope: 5; y-intercept: $(0,2)$
4. Slope: $-\dfrac{4}{3}$; y-intercept: $(0, \dfrac{1}{3})$
5. E
6. B
7. No
8. Yes
9. Remainder = 6
10. Remainder = 2
11. D
12. C
13. E
14. A
15. E
16. 3rd degree
17. 5th degree
18. Zeros: $-4, -4, -4, -4, -4, 2, 2$
19. Zeros: -2, $-\dfrac{1}{2}$, 3
20. Zeros: $-\sqrt{2}$, $\sqrt{2}$, 2
21. E
22. A
23. 10 minutes; 20 minutes

Practice 15
a. C
b. C
c. D
d. B
e. E
f. 4 seconds

Problem Set 15
1. True
2. True
3. False
4. C
5. A
6. Remainder = -2
7. Remainder = 5

8. E
9. B
10. 6th degree
11. 4th degree
12. D
13. B
14. E
15. E
16. A
17. C
18. A
19. B
20. A
21. C
22. D
23. 6 seconds

22. D
23. 2 shipments

Practice 16
a. E
b. E
c. Zero: -2 ;
    Local minimum: $(2.12, \ -4.06)$
d. $y = -90,089$
e. B
f. 3 employees

Problem Set 16
1. False
2. False
3. D
4. B
5. E
6. B
7. D
8. A
9. Zero: -2 ;
    Local maximum: $(-1.55, \ 0.63)$
10. Zero: -0.5 ;
    Local minimum: $(1.60, \ -2.62)$
11. Zero: -3 ;
    Local minimum: $(0.29, \ -6.30)$
12. $y = 4,323$
13. $y = 37,865$
14. C
15. A
16. C
17. C
18. B
19. E
20. D
21. A

CHAPTER 3

Practice 17

a. D
b. Vertical asymptotes: $x = 0$ and $x = -2$
c. Zero: $x = 2$
d. B
e. Zeros: $-2, 1, 5$
f. $3.60 per doll

Problem Set 17

1. True
2. False
3. C
4. D
5. B
6. C
7. C
8. Vertical asymptote: $x = 3$
9. Vertical asymptotes: $x = -2$ and $x = 2$
10. Vertical asymptotes: $x = -1$ and $x = 4$
11. Vertical asymptote: $x = -2$
12. Vertical asymptote: $x = \dfrac{3}{2}$
13. Vertical asymptotes: $x = 0$ and $x = 5$
14. Largest zero: $x = 2$
15. Smallest zero: $x = -2.65$
16. $y = 3,395$
17. $y = -82$
18. A
19. B
20. E
21. Zeros: $-7, -7, -3, 5, 5, 5$
22. Zeros: $-4, 3, 6$
23. $64.50 per processor

Practice 18

a. No vertical asymptote
b. Horizontal asymptote: $y = -2$
c. D
d. D
e. Zeros: $-\sqrt{7},\ -2,\ \sqrt{7}$
f. 7.29 pounds

Problem Set 18

1. True
2. True
3. False
4. B
5. C

6. Vertical asymptote: $x = -\dfrac{1}{2}$
7. Vertical asymptotes: $x = -3$ and $x = 3$
8. No vertical asymptote
9. Horizontal asymptote: $y = 0$
10. Horizontal asymptote: $y = 3$
11. B
12. Yes
13. No
14. A
15. C
16. Zero: -0.5 ;
    Local Maximum: $(0.80, 18.30)$
17. Zero: 2;
    Local Minimum: $(0.64,\ -1.64)$
18. E
19. D
20. E
21. Zeros: $-5,\ -5,\ -2,\ -2,\ -2,\ -2, 1$
22. Zeros: $-\sqrt{5},\ \sqrt{5}, 3$
23. 2.8 pounds

Practice 19

a. Vertical asymptotes: $x = -1$, $x = 3$
b. Horizontal asymptote: $y = 0$
c. C
d. C
e. B
f. 20 feet

Problem Set 19

1. False
2. False
3. Vertical asymptotes: $x = -3$, $x = 3$;
   Horizontal asymptote: $y = -2$
4. Vertical asymptotes: $x = -2$, $x = 1$;
   Horizontal asymptote: $y = 2$
5. Vertical asymptote: $x = 4$
6. Vertical asymptotes: $x = -\dfrac{1}{2}$, $x = 5$
7. Vertical asymptotes: $x = -1$, $x = 2$
8. Horizontal asymptote: $y = 0$
9. Horizontal asymptote: $y = 2$
10. A
11. C
12. D
13. A

14. B
15. C
16. E
17. C
18. A
19. $y = 3,047$
20. $y = 347,258$
21. Zeros: -4, 3
22. Zeros: -1, 2, 2
23. 30 feet

Practice 20

a. x-intercept: $(2,0)$

b. Horizontal asymptote: $y = \dfrac{3}{2}$

c. A
d. B
e. C
f. 6.32 seconds

Problem Set 20

1. True
2. True
3. C
4. x-intercept: $(3,0)$
5. C
6. C
7. B
8. E
9. D
10. Horizontal asymptote: $y = 3$
11. D
12. A
13. E
14. C
15. E
16. C
17. A
18. A
19. B
20. C
21. D
22. B
23. 3.56 seconds

Practice 21

a. A
b. B
c. D
d. E

e. C
f. 80 feet

Problem Set 21

1. True
2. True
3. Yes
4. No
5. Vertical asymptotes: $x = -3$, $x = 3$
6. Vertical asymptotes: $x = -1$, $x = 5$
7. Horizontal asymptote: $y = -2$
8. B
9. Horizontal asymptote: $y = 4$
10. E
11. C
12. D
13. C
14. E
15. A
16. B
17. B
18. C
19. D
20. A
21. E
22. B
23. 176 feet

Practice 22

a. D
b. E
c. E
d. A
e. $x = -4.61, 2.61$
f. $k = 0.33$

Problem Set 22

1. True
2. True
3. Vertical asymptotes: $x = -\sqrt{2}$, $x = \sqrt{2}$
4. Vertical asymptotes: $x = -2$, $x = 1$
5. Horizontal asymptote: $y = 0$
6. E
7. B
8. C
9. A
10. C
11. D
12. C
13. D
14. B
15. E

16. B
17. A
18. D
19. E
20. $x = -1.35, \ 3.35$
21. $x = -6.06, \ 0.64$
22. $x = -1.51, \ 1.07, \ 1.87$
23. $k = 1.2$

PRE-CALCULUS: ANSWER KEY & TEST BANK

CHAPTER 4

Practice 23
a. E
b. $h(0) = 1$
c. E
d. D
e. Vertical asymptote: $x = -2$;
   Horizontal asymptote: $y = 1$
f. 100 feet

Problem Set 23
1. False
2. True
3. E
4. B
5. A
6. 32
7. $\dfrac{1}{4}$
8. 1
9. C
10. A
11. D
12. D
13. B
14. B
15. Vertical asymptotes: $x = -\sqrt{2}$ and $x = \sqrt{2}$
16. Vertical asymptotes: $x = 1$ and $x = 3$
17. Horizontal asymptote: $y = -2$
18. D
19. C
20. Vertical asymptote: $x = 6$;
    Horizontal asymptote: $y = -\dfrac{1}{3}$
21. $x = -1,\ 0.5,\ 2$
22. $x = -2,\ 1$
23. 7 inches

Practice 24
a. $\dfrac{1}{9}$
b. 42.875
c. 30.25
d. E
e. C
f. 2.18 milligrams

Problem Set 24
1. True
2. True
3. A
4. B
5. 1
6. $\dfrac{1}{4}$
7. 0.75
8. 20.25
9. 9.1875
10. C
11. E
12. B
13. B
14. D
15. A
16. C
17. A
18. B
19. E
20. A
21. B
22. E
23. 0.11 milligrams

Practice 25
a. 4
b. 0.8451
c. $x = 3$
d. $x = 1.1461$
e. E
f. $13,575.65

Problem Set 25
1. True
2. True
3. Horizontal asymptote: $y = 0$
4. A
5. 4
6. 3
7. 2
8. 1.0792
9. 2.1761
10. 0.4771
11. $y = \dfrac{1}{9}$
12. $x = 2$
13. $x = 0.9031$

14. $x = 1.1461$
15. B
16. $\dfrac{5}{2}$
17. D
18. E
19. D
20. B
21. B
22. E
23. $24,702.31

Practice 26

a. $x = 6$
b. $x = -\dfrac{5}{2}$
c. 1.8271
d. $x = -0.2871$
e. $x = 0.5391$
f. 4.19 years

Problem Set 26

1. True
2. False
3. 5
4. 8
5. 7
6. 0.6021
7. 0.9542
8. $x = \dfrac{1}{2}$
9. $x = 4$
10. $x = 1$
11. $y = \dfrac{1}{3}$
12. $x = -\dfrac{5}{2}$
13. $x = 1.1761$
14. 2.3219
15. 2.0959
16. 1.7737
17. $x = 1.7712$
18. $x = -0.0754$
19. $x = 2.2153$
20. C
21. A
22. D
23. A
24. 18.85 years

Practice 27

a. B
b. C
c. D
d. 4
e. C
f. 16,307 people

Problem Set 27

1. True
2. False
3. $x = -\dfrac{2}{3}$
4. $x = 11$
5. 1
6. B
7. $x = 1.3652$
8. $x = -0.4406$
9. $x = 0.4654$
10. A
11. E
12. D
13. C
14. E
15. E
16. 3
17. 0
18. 6
19. B
20. D
21. A
22. E
23. 29,937 people

Practice 28

a. E
b. D
c. C
d. $x = -1, 3$
e. $x = 4.8456$
f. 23.36 years

Problem Set 28

1. True
2. False
3. A
4. D
5. D
6. A
7. C
8. E
9. 3.1699

10. 1.4650
11. −3.8074
12. E
13. B
14. C
15. B
16. $x = 32$
17. $x = \dfrac{9}{2}$
18. $x = 0, \dfrac{5}{2}$
19. $x = 3.1623$
20. $x = 1.8377$
21. C
22. A
23. 5.93 months

Practice 29
a. 137.68
b. A
c. $x = 2$ ($x = -4$ extraneous)
d. B
e. D
f. 351 people

Problem Set 29
1. False
2. True
3. 20.09
4. 2.72
5. 1,299.6
6. 165.26
7. D
8. E
9. B
10. A
11. $x = \dfrac{1}{81}$
12. $x = -\dfrac{28}{3}$
13. $x = 1$ ($x = -7$ extraneous)
14. $x = -2.6102, 2.6102$
15. $x = 3.7783$
16. B
17. D
18. A
19. C
20. C
21. B
22. E
23. 441 people

Practice 30
a. 2.48
b. $x = 10.1589$
c. E
d. $x = 4$ ($x = -1$ extraneous)
e. B
f. $897.50

Problem Set 30
1. True
2. True
3. 20.09
4. 1.79
5. 911.06
6. 1.5
7. 1.2770
8. B
9. A
10. $x = 1.6094$
11. $x = -0.3153$
12. $x = 11.5835$
13. C
14. E
15. D
16. $x = 2$
17. $x = 5.2945$
18. $x = 3$ ($x = -2$ extraneous)
19. C
20. D
21. D
22. A
23. $2,254.99

CHAPTER 5

Practice 31
a. E
b. 0.21
c. E
d. $x = 9$ ($x = 6$ is extraneous)
e. $x = 8$
f. $14,772.44

Problem Set 31
1. True
2. False
3. True
4. $x = 0.3770$
5. $x = 4.8330$
6. C
7. A
8. D
9. 0.43
10. D
11. E
12. E
13. $t = -1$
14. $x = -3$ ($x = -6$ is extraneous)
15. $x = 3.5$
16. $x = 71$
17. $x = 3$
18. $x = -1.6838$
19. $x = 1.2840$
20. C
21. B
22. $9,547.64

Practice 32
a. $t = 316.2$
b. $x = \dfrac{56}{3}$
c. D
d. C
e. C
f. 150 feet

Problem Set 32
1. False
2. False
3. $x = 5$
4. $x = 2$ ($x = -2$ is extraneous)
5. $x = 215.4$
6. $t = 1,000$
7. $x = 2, 4$

8. E
9. D
10. $x = -\dfrac{7}{5}$ (or $x = -1.4$)
11. $t = 1$ ($t = -6$ is extraneous)
12. $x = 4$
13. $x = 0$
14. A
15. D
16. D
17. E
18. B
19. E
20. C
21. B
22. E
23. 125 feet

Practice 33
a. B
b. C
c. $x = 16$
d. A
e. $x = 5$
f. 125 cubic inches

Problem Set 33
1. False
2. True
3. 1.8614
4. -0.9102
5. D
6. D
7. B
8. A
9. B
10. $x = 27$
11. $x = -8, 8$
12. $x = 32$
13. B
14. E
15. $x = 13$
16. No valid solution ($x = -6, \ -5$ are extraneous)
17. $x = 9$
18. $x = 2$
19. A
20. C
21. D
22. A
23. 27 cubic inches

Practice 34

a. E
b. $x = 75$
c. $x = 2$ ($x = -3$ is extraneous)
d. $y = 2$
e. $4{,}000$ N

Problem Set 34

1. False
2. True
3. A
4. B
5. B
6. D
7. C
8. B
9. $x = -3$
10. $x = 21$
11. $x = 81$
12. $x = 36$
13. $x = 6$
14. $x = -4$ ($x = -7$ is extraneous)
15. $y = 72$
16. $y = 8$
17. $y = 162$
18. B
19. E
20. $2{,}000$ N
21. 16 inches

Practice 35

a. $c = -3$
b. 166
c. 58.75
d. $x = 5$
e. $x = 1.6$
f. A

Problem Set 35

1. True
2. True
3. C
4. $c = 7$
5. 0.5
6. 101
7. $y = 8$
8. 4.25
9. B
10. A
11. D
12. $y = 48$

13. $y = 1$
14. A
15. C
16. E
17. $x = 27$
18. $x = 2$
19. $x = 3$ ($x = -3$ is extraneous)
20. $x = 1.08$
21. $x = 1.5$
22. C
23. $86.36

Practice 36

a. C
b. $f(1.25) = 6$
c. B
d. $y = 8$
e. $x = -\dfrac{4}{3}, 0$
f. $1.55

Problem Set 36

1. True
2. False
3. B
4. A
5. E
6. $f(4) = 9$
7. $f(-6) = -24$
8. $f(1.25) = 3$
9. C
10. E
11. D
12. $y = 192$
13. $y = 5$
14. $x = -8, -2$
15. $x = -1, 0$
16. $x = 8$ ($x = 2$ is extraneous)
17. $x = -5, 5$
18. $x = 3{,}125$
19. C
20. A
21. $6.00

CHAPTER 6

Practice 37

a. $\sin F = 0.481$; $\cos F = 0.877$; $\tan F = 0.549$

b. 21.856

c. $y = -9$

d. $y = -100$

e. 13.595 feet

Problem Set 37

1. True
2. False
3. E
4. A
5. C
6. $\sin C = 0.385$; $\cos C = 0.923$; $\tan C = 0.417$
7. $\sin I = 0.406$; $\cos I = 0.915$; $\tan I = 0.443$
8. $\sin N = 0.772$; $\cos N = 0.635$; $\tan N = 1.217$
9. $\sin P = 0.839$; $\cos P = 0.540$; $\tan P = 1.552$
10. 0.423
11. 59.102 inches
12. 17.061 centimeters
13. E
14. C
15. $y = 2$
16. $y = -1$
17. $y = -48$
18. $y = 4$
19. 0.2
20. 6
21. D
22. B
23. 16.178 feet

Practice 38

a. 91.3125°

b. 1.0063

c. 81.411 meters

d. D

e. 235.165 feet

Problem Set 38

1. True
2. True
3. $\sin R = 0.909$; $\cos R = 0.422$; $\tan R = 2.154$
4. $\sin K = 0.741$; $\cos K = 0.673$; $\tan K = 1.101$
5. 18.4°
6. 63.715°
7. 0.3249
8. 1.2489
9. 1.2655
10. 40.068 feet
11. 98.351 inches
12. 30.213 meters
13. 6.54
14. 2, −2
15. 81
16. C
17. E
18. 1.65
19. 0.43
20. $x = 3$ ($x = -7$ is extraneous)
21. $x = -\dfrac{1}{3}$, 1
22. $t = 5$
23. 7.820 feet

Practice 39

a. $\csc 45° = \sqrt{2}$, $\sin 60° = \dfrac{\sqrt{3}}{2}$, $\tan 30° = \dfrac{1}{\sqrt{3}}$

b. 120.1 meters

c. $\theta = 35°$

d. $FG = 54.6$, $\angle F = 27.0°$, $\angle G = 63.0°$

e. 30°

Problem Set 39

1. True
2. False
3. −1.2538
4. 1.0091
5. $\tan 45° = \dfrac{1}{1}$, $\sin 45° = \dfrac{1}{\sqrt{2}}$, $\sec 45° = \dfrac{\sqrt{2}}{1}$
6. $\sin 30° = \dfrac{1}{2}$, $\cos 30° = \dfrac{\sqrt{3}}{2}$, $\tan 60° = \dfrac{\sqrt{3}}{1}$
7. 47.302 yards
8. 3.993 decimeters
9. 130.2 meters
10. $\theta = 56.3°$
11. $\alpha = -76.7°$
12. $\alpha = 59.4°$
13. $\theta = 78.1°$
14. $\alpha = 72.9°$
15. $\theta = 58.5°$
16. $DE = 65.9$, $EF = 47.9$, $\angle D = 36°$
17. $QR = 44.7$, $PR = 42.0$, $\angle Q = 70°$
18. $GH = 46.6$, $\angle G = 64.9°$, $\angle H = 25.1°$
19. E

20. C
21. A
22. D
23. 38.0°

Practice 40

a. $a = 14.1$
b. $\alpha = 84°$
c. $x = 5.65$
d. 1.38
e. 34.99
f. 20 miles

Problem Set 40

1. True
2. True
3. 6.2 meters
4. 163.88 yards
5. $\theta = 60°$
6. $\theta = 30°$
7. $\alpha = 45°$
8. $\alpha = 30°$
9. $a = 8.4$
10. $b = 6.6$
11. $c = 13.3$
12. $\alpha = 73.8°$
13. $\theta = 69.9°$
14. $\alpha = 75.2°$
15. $IK = 23.6, HK = 14.5, \angle K = 52°$
16. $TR = 27.5, \angle T = 68.0°, \angle R = 22.0°$
17. $x = 4.88$
18. $x = 9$ ($x = 2$ is extraneous)
19. E
20. A
21. 0.48
22. 32.56
23. 17 miles

Practice 41

a. $\alpha = 60°$
b. $m = 28.7$
c. $c = 40.2$
d. $\theta = 35.4°$
e. E
f. 14.00 feet

Problem Set 41

1. True
2. True
3. $x = -1.72, 2.72$

4. $x = -2.16, 1.16, 5$
5. $\alpha = 45°$
6. $\theta = 30°$
7. $\alpha = 45°$
8. 48 meters
9. 80.3 inches
10. $a = 23.9$
11. $q = 22.5$
12. $\theta = 66.7°$
13. $\alpha = 49.5°$
14. $c = 8.5$
15. $a = 22.3$
16. $\alpha = 20.1°$
17. $\theta = 23.7°$
18. 60°
19. 0.92
20. 3.4
21. B
22. D
23. 20.98 feet

CHAPTER 7

Practice 42
a. $\alpha = 540°$
b. $\theta = 22.3°$
c. B
d. 3.8
e. 25.37°

Problem Set 42
1. True
2. True
3. A
4. C
5. $\alpha = 180°$
6. $\alpha = 270°$
7. $\alpha = 450°$
8. $\alpha = 330°$
9. $\theta = 30°$
10. $\theta = 60°$
11. 43.691 feet
12. 102.936 meters
13. $b = 6.1$
14. $a = 21.2$
15. $b = 20.4$
16. $\alpha = 80.6°$
17. $\theta = 56.6°$
18. $\alpha = 23.0°$
19. E
20. -1.125
21. 7
22. 11.27
23. 25.66°

Practice 43
a. C
b. E
c. D
d. $e = 31.0$
e. 88.2
f. 69.31 days

Problem Set 43
1. True
2. True
3. $\alpha = 630°$
4. $\alpha = 225°$
5. D
6. C
7. B
8. A

9. E
10. C
11. C
12. A
13. E
14. D
15. $q = 32.7$
16. $a = 41.4$
17. $\theta = 81.3°$
18. $\alpha = 25.9°$
19. B
20. C
21. 16
22. 128
23. 115.13 days

Practice 44
a. $\dfrac{3\pi}{5}$
b. 150°
c. 0.43
d. E
e. 71 miles per hour

Problem Set 44
1. True
2. False
3. $\alpha = -40°$
4. $\alpha = 145°$
5. C
6. A
7. E
8. D
9. B
10. E
11. $\dfrac{\pi}{4}$
12. $\dfrac{\pi}{2}$
13. $\dfrac{2\pi}{3}$
14. 30°
15. 135°
16. 286.5°
17. 0.87
18. -1
19. 0.59
20. B
21. E

22. C
23. B
24. 15.71 feet per second

Practice 45

a. Amplitude: 3, Period: 8, Midline: $y = 2$
b. B
c. D
d. A
e. 50 feet

Problem Set 45

1. True
2. True
3. E
4. D
5. 0.98
6. 0.92
7. $\dfrac{3\pi}{4}$
8. $\dfrac{5\pi}{6}$
9. 60°
10. 210°
11. Amplitude: 2, Period: 2π, Midline: $y = 0$
12. Amplitude: 3, Period: 2, Midline: $y = -2$
13. Amplitude: 4, Period: 4, Midline: $y = 1$
14. A
15. D
16. C
17. -1
18. 2
19. C
20. E
21. A
22. E
23. 145 feet

Practice 46

a. D
b. A
c. E
d. $\dfrac{16}{3}$
e. 10 amps

Problem Set 46

1. True
2. False
3. True

4. Period = 4, Amplitude = 0.39, Horizontal shift = 0
5. Period $= \dfrac{1}{30}$, Amplitude = 220, Horizontal shift $= \dfrac{1}{180}$
6. Period = 12, Amplitude = 24.8, Horizontal shift $= \dfrac{9}{2}$
7. C
8. B
9. E
10. D
11. A
12. E
13. C
14. A
15. B
16. E
17. C
18. E
19. B
20. 14
21. $\dfrac{13}{2}$
22. 8 amps

Practice 47

a. C
b. E
c. B
d. 3
e. 0.7

Problem Set 47

1. False
2. True
3. D
4. A
5. 0.31
6. 0.38
7. $\theta = 120°$
8. $\theta = 30°$
9. E
10. B
11. D
12. A
13. D
14. A
15. D
16. B
17. A

18. B
19. 9.91
20. 2
21. E
22. 0.5

Practice 48

a. Periodic
b. 0.86
c. D
d. C
e. B
f. −1.1 inches

Problem Set 48

1. False
2. True
3. B
4. A
5. C
6. Periodic
7. Periodic
8. Periodic
9. 1.02
10. −6.36
11. −0.74
12. 1.47
13. B
14. A
15. A
16. E
17. A
18. E
19. 2 roots
20. D
21. E
22. −0.27 inches

Practice 49

a. $-\dfrac{\pi}{3}$
b. $\dfrac{\pi}{4}$
c. E
d. B
e. D
f. 2 meters

Problem Set 49

1. True
2. True

3. Periodic
4. Non-periodic
5. 0.73
6. −0.32
7. $\dfrac{\pi}{2}$
8. $-\dfrac{\pi}{6}$
9. E
10. $\dfrac{\pi}{6}$
11. E
12. B
13. D
14. A
15. C
16. B
17. E
18. C
19. 1
20. B
21. $\dfrac{\pi}{220}$
22. B
23. 3.5 meters

Practice 50

a. B
b. A
c. $x = 1.04,\ 3.67$
d. $x = 1.34,\ 3.90$
e. E
f. 0.75 seconds

Problem Set 50

1. False
2. False
3. 2.47
4. 0.81
5. $-\dfrac{\pi}{4}$
6. $\dfrac{\pi}{6}$
7. D
8. A
9. C
10. E
11. B
12. C

13. $x = \dfrac{\pi}{3}, \dfrac{2\pi}{3}$

14. $x = \dfrac{\pi}{3}, \dfrac{5\pi}{3}$

15. $x = 1.79, \ 3.23$

16. $x = 0.58, \ 4.13$

17. $x = -2, \ 1, \ 3$

18. E

19. A

20. 3 times

21. $\dfrac{\pi}{3}$

22. D

23. 1.5 seconds

CHAPTER 8

Practice 51
a. A
b. $x = 0.32,\ 3.46$
c. $x = \dfrac{7\pi}{10}$
d. C
e. 1.11
f. 4 minutes

Problem Set 51
1. True
2. True
3. $-\dfrac{\pi}{4}$
4. 0
5. B
6. D
7. D
8. A
9. E
10. $x = 0.46,\ 3.61$
11. $x = \dfrac{3\pi}{4}$
12. $x = 0.10,\ 1.47,\ 3.24,\ 4.61$
13. $x = 2.74,\ 5.63$
14. C
15. A
16. E
17. D
18. A
19. C
20. 9.57
21. B
22. 2 minutes

Practice 52
a. $\theta = 57°36'$
b. $x = \dfrac{4\pi}{3}$
c. $x = \pi,\ \dfrac{3\pi}{2}$
d. E
e. $\tan\theta = -\dfrac{5}{8}$
f. $37.89

Problem Set 52
1. True
2. True
3. D
4. E
5. $\alpha = 40°$
6. $\theta = 25°32'$
7. $x = \dfrac{\pi}{2}$
8. $x = \dfrac{\pi}{6},\ \dfrac{\pi}{2}$
9. C
10. A
11. B
12. E
13. D
14. C
15. A
16. $\cos\alpha = \dfrac{2}{7}$
17. $\tan\theta = -\dfrac{4}{5}$
18. $\dfrac{5\pi}{12}$
19. $x = 12$
20. B
21. D
22. $24.87

Practice 53
a. E
b. D
c. $\dfrac{5\cos\alpha\sec\alpha}{\csc\alpha} = 2$
d. Yes
e. 2 hours

Problem Set 53
1. True
2. False
3. $x = 2.15,\ 4.67$
4. $x = 1.37,\ 4.51$
5. $\theta = 60°$
6. $\alpha = 18°30'$
7. B
8. D
9. E

10. C
11. B
12. E
13. A
14. $\sec\theta = 4$
15. $\dfrac{4\cos\alpha\sec\alpha}{\csc\alpha} = 3$
16. Yes
17. No
18. -5
19. D
20. C
21. E
22. 1 hour

Practice 54
a. B
b. A
c. B
d. $\cos(x-y) = \dfrac{171}{221}$
e. $6.12°$

Problem Set 54
1. False
2. True
3. C
4. D
5. D
6. A
7. C
8. B
9. E
10. D
11. $\sin\theta = \dfrac{2}{5}$
12. $\cot\alpha = 3$
13. C
14. E
15. B
16. $\sin(x+y) = \dfrac{24}{25}$
17. $\cos(x-y) = \dfrac{204}{325}$
18. D
19. -1.3
20. A
21. 3 real roots
22. $8.21°$

Practice 55
a. C
b. E
c. A
d. $\tan(x+y) = \dfrac{14}{5}$
e. 35.65 hours

Problem Set 55
1. False
2. False
3. D
4. C
5. $\theta = 61°$
6. $\alpha = 19°$
7. B
8. D
9. E
10. C
11. A
12. D
13. E
14. C
15. $\cos(x+y) = \dfrac{33}{65}$
16. $\tan(x-y) = -\dfrac{8}{27}$
17. $\tan(x+y) = -\dfrac{34}{27}$
18. $k = 7$
19. B
20. 3.5
21. 7.8 cm
22. 33.18 hours

Practice 56
a. B
b. E
c. C
d. $\cos 2\alpha = -\dfrac{23}{25}$
e. C
f. $32.98

Problem Set 56
1. True
2. False
3. D
4. C
5. C

6. A
7. B
8. E
9. D
10. $\sin(x+y) = \dfrac{84}{85}$
11. $\cos(x-y) = \dfrac{4}{5}$
12. $\tan(x+y) = \dfrac{26}{7}$
13. $\sin 2\theta = \dfrac{24}{25}$
14. $\cos 2\alpha = \dfrac{1}{8}$
15. $\tan 2\theta = -\dfrac{12}{5}$
16. A
17. B
18. E
19. 7
20. Vertical asymptotes: $x = 3$, $x = -3$
    Horizontal asymptotes: $y = -5$
21. D
22. $44.96

Practice 57
a. D
b. C
c. E
d. $\tan \dfrac{\theta}{2} = \dfrac{1}{7}$
e. C
f. 14.69 inches

Problem Set 57
1. True
2. True
3. D
4. A
5. D
6. B
7. E
8. C
9. B
10. $\sin 2\alpha = \dfrac{120}{169}$
11. $\cos 2\theta = -\dfrac{17}{25}$

12. $\sin \dfrac{\alpha}{2} = \dfrac{2}{3}$
13. $\cos \dfrac{\alpha}{2} = -\dfrac{1}{4}$
14. $\tan \dfrac{\theta}{2} = \dfrac{3}{5}$
15. E
16. A
17. C
18. D
19. $\dfrac{1}{3}$
20. π
21. 5
22. 1.47 inches

Practice 58
a. C
b. $x = \dfrac{\pi}{3}$
c. $x = \dfrac{\pi}{6}$
d. E
e. 6.99

Problem Set 58
1. True
2. True
3. D
4. B
5. A
6. E
7. A
8. C
9. $\cos \dfrac{\alpha}{2} = \dfrac{3}{4}$
10. $\sin \dfrac{\alpha}{2} = -\dfrac{4}{5}$
11. $x = \dfrac{\pi}{6}, \dfrac{\pi}{2}, \dfrac{5\pi}{6}$
12. $x = \dfrac{2\pi}{3}$
13. $x = \dfrac{\pi}{2}$
14. $x = \dfrac{\pi}{4}$
15. E
16. C
17. B

18. D

19. $x = -\dfrac{1}{3}$

20. 6

21. Amplitude = 4

22. 7.05

CHAPTER 9

Practice 59

a. $m_x = -8$, $m_y = 3$, $\|\mathbf{m}\| = 8.54$

b. $\mathbf{q} - \mathbf{p} = (5, -1)$

c. $x = \dfrac{\pi}{3}$

d. $x = 0, \dfrac{\pi}{3}, \dfrac{2\pi}{3}, \pi$

e. B

f. 100 yards

Problem Set 59

1. True
2. True
3. $u_x = 4$, $u_y = 3$, $\|\mathbf{u}\| = 5$
4. $PQ_x = -5$, $PQ_y = -5$, $\|\overrightarrow{PQ}\| = 7.07$
5. $k_x = 6$, $k_y = 3$, $\|\mathbf{k}\| = 6.71$
6. $\mathbf{u} + \mathbf{v} = (-1, 7)$
7. $\mathbf{m} - \mathbf{n} = (-5, -4)$
8. $\mathbf{q} - \mathbf{p} = (3, 3)$
9. $\theta = 42°$
10. $\alpha = 13°30'$
11. A
12. D
13. A
14. E
15. $x = \dfrac{\pi}{6}, \dfrac{5\pi}{6}$
16. $x = \dfrac{2\pi}{3}$
17. $x = 0, \dfrac{\pi}{4}, \dfrac{3\pi}{4}, \pi$
18. E
19. D
20. $g(2) = -6$
21. 12
22. 40 feet

Practice 60

a. $4\mathbf{v} - 3\mathbf{w} = 29\mathbf{i} + (-29\mathbf{j})$

b. $\|\mathbf{u}\| = 17.5$; $\theta = 66.4°$

c. E

d. B

e. E

f. $p_x = -27.5$, $p_y = -47.6$

Problem Set 60

1. True
2. True
3. $u_x = -2$, $u_y = 6$, $\|\mathbf{u}\| = 6.32$
4. $v_x = -8$, $v_y = -5$, $\|\mathbf{v}\| = 9.43$
5. $2\mathbf{v} = 4\mathbf{i} + (-6\mathbf{j})$
6. $3\mathbf{v} - 2\mathbf{w} = 14\mathbf{i} + (-21\mathbf{j})$
7. $\|\mathbf{w}\| = 7.21$
8. $w_x = 2$, $w_y = 3.5$
9. $\|\mathbf{u}\| = 16.2$, $\theta = 68.2°$
10. $-\dfrac{5}{13}\mathbf{i} + \dfrac{12}{13}\mathbf{j}$
11. E
12. D
13. $\cot(-\theta) = \dfrac{1}{2}$
14. $\cos\alpha \cot\alpha + \sin\alpha = \dfrac{7}{4}$
15. $x = 0, \dfrac{\pi}{4}$
16. $x = \dfrac{2\pi}{3}$
17. B
18. E
19. C
20. $x = 16$
21. $\dfrac{b}{a} = 1.25$
22. $s_x = -24.75$, $s_y = 24.75$

Practice 61

a. $\|\mathbf{p}\| = 28.5$; $\theta = 108.4°$

b. $\dfrac{7}{25}\mathbf{i} - \dfrac{24}{25}\mathbf{j}$

c. $88.79\mathbf{i} + 23.79\mathbf{j}$

d. $x = \dfrac{\pi}{6}, \dfrac{5\pi}{6}$

e. E

f. 1,720.45 foot-pounds

Problem Set 61

1. True
2. True

3. $-3\mathbf{k} = 9\mathbf{i} - 21\mathbf{j}$

4. $\frac{1}{2}\mathbf{h} - 2\mathbf{k} = 8\mathbf{i} - 10\mathbf{j}$

5. $\|\mathbf{k}\| = 7.62$

6. $v_x = 8.5$, $v_y = 8.5$

7. $\|\mathbf{w}\| = 32.4$; $\theta = 98.9°$

8. $\frac{15}{17}\mathbf{i} - \frac{8}{17}\mathbf{j}$

9. $195.57\mathbf{i} + 72.93\mathbf{j}$

10. 10.2 m/s

11. $96.57\mathbf{i} - 12.71\mathbf{j}$

12. C

13. A

14. $x = 0$

15. $x = \frac{\pi}{6}, \frac{\pi}{2}, \frac{5\pi}{6}$

16. A

17. D

18. $f(\log_5 \frac{1}{125}) = \frac{1}{64}$

19. $f^{-1}(5.5) = 0.92$

20. 8,250,000 joules

21. 4,095.76 joules

22. 866.03 foot-pounds

Practice 62

a. $\|\mathbf{r}\| = 48.4$, $\theta = 172.9°$

b. $\frac{\pi}{6}$

c. $x = \frac{\pi}{6}, \frac{\pi}{2}, \frac{5\pi}{6}$

d. D

e. C

f. 422.94 feet

Problem Set 62

1. True

2. True

3. $3\mathbf{m} - 5\mathbf{n} = 31\mathbf{i} - 7\mathbf{j}$

4. $\|-2\mathbf{n}\| = 10.20$

5. $p_x = 4.9$, $p_y = 34.7$

6. $\|\mathbf{q}\| = 35.4$, $\theta = 171.9°$

7. 108.8 mph; 18.0° south of east

8. 186.3 foot-pounds

9. $\frac{1}{2}$

10. $\frac{\pi}{3}$

11. $x = \frac{\pi}{4}, \frac{3\pi}{4}$

12. $x = 0, \frac{2\pi}{3}$

13. E

14. A

15. C

16. D

17. B

18. C

19. E

20. $\frac{4}{5}$

21. 44

22. 281.06 feet

Practice 63

a. D

b. E

c. C

d. A

e. 468.75 feet

Problem Set 63

1. True

2. True

3. $2\mathbf{m} - \frac{1}{3}\mathbf{n} = -11\mathbf{i} - 13\mathbf{j}$

4. $\|\mathbf{m} + \mathbf{n}\| = 24.08$

5. 29.0 kilometers per hour; 33.6° north of east

6. 156.2 Newtons; 26.3° north of east

7. D

8. B

9. C

10. B

11. E

12. B

13. E

14. B

15. C

16. A

17. B

18. C

19. E

20. 1.14

21. 801

22. 12.5 feet

CHAPTER 10

Practice 64

a. C

b. $\dfrac{1}{\cos^2\theta - \sin^2\theta} = \dfrac{8}{3}$

c. $x = -2,\ y = 3$

d. $x = -1,\ y = 4$

e. E

f. 125 small, 376 large

Problem Set 64

1. True
2. True
3. B
4. D
5. E
6. C
7. A
8. D
9. $\cot\theta = \dfrac{1}{4}$
10. $\dfrac{1}{\cos^2\alpha - \sin^2\alpha} = \dfrac{7}{6}$
11. $x = 3,\ y = 5$
12. $x = 2,\ y = -4$
13. $x = 5,\ y = 2$
14. $x = 3,\ y = -1$
15. $x = -2,\ y = 3$
16. E
17. E
18. B
19. $\sqrt{x^2 + y^2} = 4$
20. $\|\mathbf{v}\| = 13.42$
21. $\alpha = 30°,\ 150°$
22. 1,200 children tickets, 1,010 adult tickets

Practice 65

a. C

b. $(4,1),\ (1,-2)$

c. $x = 7,\ y = -1,\ z = 1$

d. $(-1.97, 3.48),\ (0.96, 3.88)$

e. $g\!\left(f\!\left(\dfrac{\pi}{12} \right) \right) = \dfrac{\pi}{12}$

f. 456 children tickets, 251 senior tickets, and 1,414 adult tickets

Problem Set 65

1. True
2. False
3. $h_x = 14.1,\ h_y = -5.1$
4. $\|\mathbf{k}\| = 34.7,\ \theta = 191.6°$
5. 277.8 kilometers per hour, 49.2° south of east
6. 4,178.3 Newtons
7. D
8. A
9. B
10. E
11. Inconsistent
12. $x = \dfrac{1}{3},\ y = -\dfrac{1}{2}$
13. $(3,1),\ (1,-1)$
14. $x = -2,\ y = 2,\ z = 4$
15. $x = 3,\ y = -1$
16. $(-1.85, 2.36),\ (0,3)$
17. C
18. E
19. 48.19°
20. $x = 43.72$
21. $g\!\left(f\!\left(\dfrac{\pi}{9} \right) \right) = \dfrac{\pi}{9}$
22. 50 Choconut Bars, 75 Almond-Bliss Bars, and 375 Fudge-Brownie Bars

Practice 66

a. $(0,0),\ (2,36)$

b. $x = 2,\ y = 5,\ z = 1$

c. $x = 4,\ y = 3$

d. C

e. B

f. 601 feet

Problem Set 66

1. False
2. True
3. $3\mathbf{u} - 2\mathbf{v} = -49\mathbf{i} + 93\mathbf{j}$
4. $\|\mathbf{u} + \mathbf{v}\| = 17.46$
5. A
6. C
7. $(2,3),\ (-3,-7)$
8. $(0,0),\ (2,32)$
9. $x = -6,\ y = -4,\ z = 7$

10. $x = -3, \ y = 3$

11. $(-0.8, -3.8), \ (1.6, -3.5)$

12. $x = 2, \ y = -4$

13. $x = 5, \ y = 2$

14. D

15. E

16. A

17. $x = \dfrac{\pi}{4}, \ \dfrac{3\pi}{4}$

18. $x = 0, \ \dfrac{\pi}{3}$

19. B

20. E

21. D

22. 11 feet

Practice 67

a. $(-5, -2), (5, 2)$

b. -14

c. $x = -2, \ y = 1, \ z = 4$

d. $\cos\theta + \cos\theta\tan^2\theta = \dfrac{7}{4}$

e. 1,280 joules

Problem Set 67

1. True

2. False

3. $\|\mathbf{m}\| = 58.7, \ \theta = 13.8°$

4. $\dfrac{24}{25}\mathbf{i} - \dfrac{7}{25}\mathbf{j}$

5. Dependent

6. $(-1, -4), (4, 6)$

7. $(-4, -3), (4, 3)$

8. -30

9. -51

10. $x = 7, \ y = -2$

11. $x = \dfrac{1}{3}, \ y = \dfrac{1}{2}$

12. $x = -2, \ y = 1, \ z = 3$

13. $\sin\left(\dfrac{\pi}{2} - \theta\right) = \dfrac{1}{3}$

14. $\sin\alpha + \sin\alpha\cot^2\alpha = \dfrac{5}{2}$

15. B

16. D

17. C

18. D

19. B

20. $f(g(2)) = 1.21$

21. Maximum value of $g(f(x)) = 7$

22. 0.6 atmospheres

Practice 68

a. $x = 5, \ y = -3, \ z = 4$

b. $x = 5, \ y = -4, \ z = -2$

c. $x = \dfrac{\pi}{6}, \dfrac{5\pi}{6}$

d. $\tan\theta = -0.95$

e. 25.23 feet

Problem Set 68

1. True

2. True

3. $4\mathbf{t} - 6\mathbf{s} = -36\mathbf{i} - 10\mathbf{j}$

4. $\|\mathbf{t} + \mathbf{s}\| = 15.03$

5. E

6. C

7. Inconsistent

8. $(-3, 10), (4, -4)$

9. $x = 4, \ y = -2, \ z = 3$

10. 29

11. -200

12. $x = 3, \ y = -5$

13. $x = -\dfrac{1}{2}, \ y = \dfrac{3}{5}$

14. $x = 2, \ y = -1, \ z = -2$

15. $x = 1, \ y = 2, \ z = -3$

16. $x = 0, \ \dfrac{\pi}{3}, \ \dfrac{2\pi}{3}$

17. $x = 0$

18. B

19. C

20. $x = 65,538$

21. $\tan\theta = -0.29$

22. 27.77 feet

Practice 69

a. $x = 5, \ y = -3, \ z = 2$

b. $CA = \begin{bmatrix} 58 & 64 & -149 \\ -70 & 48 & 133 \end{bmatrix}$

c. $\sin\left(\alpha - \dfrac{\pi}{2}\right) = \dfrac{5}{7}$

d. B

e. 18.21°

Problem Set 69

1. False
2. True
3. E
4. D
5. $(-7,-2),(7,2)$
6. $x = 2, y = 7, z = -4$
7. $x = 4, y = -7$
8. $x = -\dfrac{1}{6}, y = \dfrac{2}{3}$
9. $x = 3, y = 1, z = 4$
10. $A + B = \begin{bmatrix} -1 & 1 & 22 \\ -4 & 9 & -9 \\ -7 & 1 & 16 \end{bmatrix}$
11. $B - A = \begin{bmatrix} 3 & -11 & 6 \\ -10 & -9 & 21 \\ 1 & -23 & 2 \end{bmatrix}$
12. $3B = \begin{bmatrix} 3 & -15 & 42 \\ -21 & 0 & 18 \\ -9 & -33 & 27 \end{bmatrix}$
13. $CA = \begin{bmatrix} 20 & 48 & -89 \\ -22 & 30 & 58 \end{bmatrix}$
14. $\sin\left(\theta - \dfrac{\pi}{2}\right) = \dfrac{3}{4}$
15. $\dfrac{1}{\sin\alpha\cos\alpha} = 3$
16. D
17. E
18. B
19. $n = -15$
20. 1,273.54
21. $k = \dfrac{1}{125}$
22. 40.54°

Problem Set 70

1. True
2. True
3. Dependent
4. $(-3,-2),(2,3)$
5. $x = 4, y = -3$
6. $x = -\dfrac{2}{3}, y = -\dfrac{1}{7}$
7. $x = 2, y = -3, z = 1$
8. $A + B = \begin{bmatrix} 8 & -7 & -1 \\ 4 & 14 & -7 \\ -1 & -7 & 5 \end{bmatrix}$
9. $A - B = \begin{bmatrix} 2 & 11 & -31 \\ -12 & 0 & 13 \\ 21 & -11 & -3 \end{bmatrix}$
10. $-2C = \begin{bmatrix} -4 & -6 & -10 \\ 8 & 0 & 14 \end{bmatrix}$
11. $CB = \begin{bmatrix} -25 & 13 & 20 \\ 65 & 22 & -88 \end{bmatrix}$
12. B
13. E
14. 10 photographs, 10 prints
15. 50 low-priced, 275 quality
16. D
17. E
18. C
19. Maximum value = 3
20. $\cos y = 0.52$
21. $f(\ln 3) = 27$
22. 189 cubic centimeters

Practice 70

a. $x = 3, y = -4, z = 2$

b. $CB = \begin{bmatrix} -110 & 59 & 312 \\ 217 & -166 & 87 \end{bmatrix}$

c. C

d. 4 regular, 9 extra special

e. A

f. 480 cubic centimeters

CHAPTER 11

Practice 71
a. $x = -5$, $y = 2$, $z = -1$
b. B
c. E
d. D
e. 3 seconds

Problem Set 71
1. True
2. True
3. C
4. B
5. $x = -3$, $y = 4$
6. $(1,-2)$, $(2,-1)$
7. $x = 2$, $y = -3$, $z = 1$
8. $M - N = \begin{bmatrix} -19 & 22 & -11 \\ -2 & -13 & 8 \\ 32 & -2 & 9 \end{bmatrix}$
9. $MN = \begin{bmatrix} -4 & 121 & -103 \\ -120 & -42 & 150 \\ -184 & 40 & 310 \end{bmatrix}$
10. D
11. A
12. E
13. E
14. D
15. C
16. B
17. E
18. B
19. $x = -\dfrac{3}{8}$
20. 9.49
21. -1
22. 3 seconds

Practice 72
a. $x = 3$, $y = -4$, $z = 2$
b. D
c. B
d. E
e. 0.001 moles per liter

Problem Set 72
1. True
2. False

3. $x = -2$, $y = 6$
4. $(-5,7)$, $(2,0)$
5. $x = \dfrac{1}{4}$, $y = -\dfrac{2}{3}$
6. $x = 3$, $y = -2$, $z = 1$
7. D
8. B
9. E
10. C
11. A
12. B
13. C
14. E
15. D
16. E
17. D
18. C
19. $c = 1.01$
20. $f(f(-27)) = -695.17$
21. $\theta = 71.08°$
22. 0.0000001 moles per liter

Practice 73
a. D
b. E
c. C
d. Slope = 1.73
e. 14.28 feet

Problem Set 73
1. True
2. True
3. $u_x = 58.3$, $u_y = -17.8$
4. $\|s\| = 50.5$, $\theta = 62.9°$
5. B
6. D
7. $-\dfrac{1}{2}M = \begin{bmatrix} -4 & 2 & -9 \\ -8 & -1 & 6 \\ 3 & -10 & -3 \end{bmatrix}$
8. $NM = \begin{bmatrix} -98 & 244 & 360 \\ 166 & -156 & -186 \end{bmatrix}$
9. C
10. A
11. D
12. E
13. C

14. B
15. A
16. E
17. B
18. E
19. $\dfrac{e}{f} = 1.56$
20. 4 points
21. Slope $= -1.73$
22. 25.64 feet

Practice 74
a. C
b. A
c. E
d. D
e. Length of major axis $= 4$
f. 19.84 centimeters

Problem Set 74
1. True
2. True
3. D
4. A
5. -11
6. 909
7. B
8. E
9. C
10. D
11. D
12. B
13. A
14. E
15. C
16. D
17. C
18. E
19. $f^{-1}(-5) = -4$
20. Radius $= 4$
21. Length of major axis $= 6$
22. 7.9 centimeters

Practice 75
a. C
b. D
c. A
d. B
e. D
f. 288π cubic centimeters

Problem Set 75
1. True
2. False
3. $x = -2, y = 4$
4. $(-4, -15), (-1, -9)$
5. $x = 3, y = -5, z = 2$
6. D
7. E
8. B
9. A
10. E
11. C
12. D
13. B
14. A
15. C
16. B
17. C
18. B
19. $k = 12$
20. $10^x = 23.2$
21. $\sin \alpha \csc \alpha = 1$
22. 36π cubic inches

Practice 76
a. D
b. B
c. A
d. B
e. 3
f. 170.8 miles per hour, 47.7° north of east

Problem Set 76
1. True
2. True
3. B
4. E
5. D
6. A
7. C
8. E
9. C
10. D
11. B
12. A
13. E
14. D
15. $x = \dfrac{\pi}{3}, \dfrac{\pi}{2}, \dfrac{2\pi}{3}$
16. $x = \dfrac{2\pi}{3}$

17. D
18. E
19. B
20. $x = 22$
21. 3
22. 189.24 miles per hour, 30.03° north of east

CHAPTER 12

Practice 77

a. $\dfrac{1}{9}, -\dfrac{1}{27}, \dfrac{1}{81}$

b. E

c. $a_7 = 12,288$

d. C

e. $\theta = 14.5°$

f. Price of a booth = $850

Problem Set 77

1. True
2. True
3. C
4. E
5. B
6. C
7. D
8. 20, 24, 28
9. 1,875, 9,375, 46,875
10. $\dfrac{1}{4}, -\dfrac{1}{8}, \dfrac{1}{16}$
11. E
12. D
13. B
14. A
15. $a_{17} = -27$
16. $a_6 = 486$
17. $r = -\dfrac{1}{4}$
18. C
19. E
20. D
21. $\alpha = 19.5°$
22. Annual cost = $5,500

Practice 78

a. E
b. Sum = 22,225
c. Converges
d. B
e. Total dividend amount = $4,377.31

Problem Set 78

1. True
2. False
3. A
4. C
5. B

6. E
7. 28, 25, 22
8. 64, 128, 256
9. C
10. D
11. $a_{14} = -75$
12. $r = 7$
13. $d = 3$
14. Sum = 1,275
15. Sum = 16,410
16. Converges
17. Diverges
18. C
19. E
20. $f(f^{-1}(3)) = 3$
21. y-intercept = 42
22. Total premium amount = $23,522.71

Practice 79

a. $a_1 = \dfrac{2}{3}$

b. $1 + \dfrac{3}{4} + \dfrac{9}{16} + \dfrac{27}{64} \ldots = 4$

c. $0.8888\ldots = \dfrac{8}{9}$

d. (1) $2^n - 1$ is valid for $n = 1$ ($2^{1-1} = 2^1 - 1$).

   (2) Assume that $2^n - 1$ works for $n = k$. That gives us $1 + 2 + 4 + \ldots + 2^{k-1} = 2^k - 1$.

   (3) Put the next term on the left and right side of the equation:
   $1 + 2 + 4 + \ldots + 2^{k-1} + 2^{(k+1)-1} = 2^k - 1 + 2^{(k+1)-1}$.

   (4) Simplify the right side:
   $1 + 2 + 4 + \ldots + 2^{k-1} + 2^{(k+1)-1} = 2^k - 1 + 2^k$.

   (5) Simplify the right side:
   $1 + 2 + 4 + \ldots + 2^{k-1} + 2^{(k+1)-1} = 2^{k+1} - 1$.

   (6) Substitute $k+1$ for n in the expression $2^n - 1$. That gives us $2^{k+1} - 1$.

   (7) These expressions are equivalent. Therefore $2^n - 1$ is valid for $n = k + 1$.

   (8) The equation is true for all positive integer values of n.

e. $a_1 = 15$

f. 630 feet

Problem Set 79

1. False
2. True

3. D
4. E
5. B
6. A
7. $a_{20} = 249$
8. $r = -4$
9. $a_1 = \dfrac{3}{4}$
10. Sum = 5,700
11. $20 + 10 + 5 + 2.5 + \ldots = 40$
12. $2 + 1 + \dfrac{1}{2} + \dfrac{1}{4} + \ldots = 4$
13. $0.2222\ldots = \dfrac{2}{9}$
14. $0.7777\ldots = \dfrac{7}{9}$

15. (1) $\dfrac{n(n+1)}{2}$ is valid for $n=1$ ($1 = \dfrac{1(1+1)}{2}$).

(2) Assume that $\dfrac{n(n+1)}{2}$ works for $n = k$.

That gives us $1+2+3+\ldots+k = \dfrac{k(k+1)}{2}$.

(3) Put the next term on the left and right side of the equation:

$1+2+3+\ldots+k+(k+1) = \dfrac{k(k+1)}{2} + (k+1)$.

(4) Simplify the right side:

$1+2+3+\ldots+k+(k+1) = \dfrac{k(k+1)+2(k+1)}{2}$.

(5) Simplify the right side:

$1+2+3+\ldots+k+(k+1) = \dfrac{k^2+3k+2}{2}$.

(6) Substitute $k+1$ for n in the expression $\dfrac{n(n+1)}{2}$. That gives us $\dfrac{(k+1)(k+2)}{2}$, which simplifies to equal $\dfrac{k^2+3k+2}{2}$.

(7) These expressions are equivalent. Therefore $\dfrac{n(n+1)}{2}$ is valid for $n = k+1$.

(8) The equation is true for all positive integer values of n.

16. B
17. B
18. C
19. Remainder = −73
20. Maximum = 4
21. $a_1 = 20$
22. 2,200 feet

Practice 80

a. $4.4444\ldots = \dfrac{40}{9}$

b. (1) $\dfrac{n(3n-1)}{2}$ is valid for $n=1$ ($1 = \dfrac{1(3-1)}{2}$).

(2) Assume that $\dfrac{n(3n-1)}{2}$ is valid for $n=k$. That gives us

$1+4+7+\ldots+(3k-2) = \dfrac{k(3k-1)}{2}$.

(3) Put the next term on the left and right side of the equation:

$1+4+7+\ldots+(3k-2)+(3(k+1)-2) =$
$\dfrac{k(3k-1)}{2} + (3(k+1)-2)$

(4) Simplify the right side:

$1+4+7+\ldots+(3k-2)+(3(k+1)-2) =$
$\dfrac{k(3k-1)}{2} + 3k+1$

(5) Simplify the right side:

$1+4+7+\ldots+(3k-2)+(3(k+1)-2) =$
$\dfrac{k(3k-1)+6k+2}{2}$

(6) Simplify the right side:

$1+4+7+\ldots+(3k-2)+(3(k+1)-2) =$
$\dfrac{3k^2+5k+2}{2}$

(7) Substitute $k+1$ for n in the expression $\dfrac{n(3n-1)}{2}$. That gives us $\dfrac{(k+1)(3(k+1)-1)}{2}$, which simplifies to equal $\dfrac{3k^2+5k+2}{2}$.

(8) These expressions are equivalent. Therefore $\dfrac{n(3n-1)}{2}$ is valid for $n = k+1$.

(9) The equation is true for all positive integer values of n.

c. $\dfrac{3}{5}$ or 0.6

d. $\dfrac{17}{25}$ or 0.68

e. 456,976,000 different security codes

Problem Set 80

1. True
2. True
3. $a_{29} = 1$

4. $g_1 = 2$

5. Sum = 80,200

6. Sum does not exist

7. $5 - \dfrac{5}{4} + \dfrac{5}{16} - \dfrac{5}{64} + \ldots = 4$

8. $0.6666\ldots = \dfrac{2}{3}$

9. $3.3333\ldots = \dfrac{10}{3}$

10. (1) $n(2n-1)$ is valid for $n = 1$ ($1 = 1(2-1)$)

 (2) Assume that $n(2n-1)$ is valid for $n = k$. That gives us
 $1 + 5 + 9 + \ldots + (4k-3) = k(2k-1)$.

 (3) Put the next term on the left and right side of the equation:
 $1 + 5 + 9 + \ldots + (4k-3) + (4(k+1)-3) =$
 $k(2k-1) + (4(k+1)-3)$

 (4) Simplify the right side:
 $1 + 5 + 9 + \ldots + (4k-3) + (4(k+1)-3) =$
 $(2k^2 - k) + (4k+4) - 3)$

 (5) Simplify the right side:
 $1 + 5 + 9 + \ldots + (4k-3) + (4(k+1)-3) =$
 $2k^2 + 3k + 1$

 (6) Substitute $k+1$ for n in the expression $n(2n-1)$. That gives us
 $(k+1)(2(k+1)-1)$, which simplifies to equal $2k^2 + 3k + 1$.

 (7) These expressions are equivalent. Therefore $n(2n-1)$ is valid for $n = k+1$.

 (8) The equation is true for all positive integer values of n.

11. $\dfrac{3}{10}$ or 0.3; $\dfrac{1}{5}$ or 0.2

12. $\dfrac{1}{36}$

13. $\dfrac{1}{9}$

14. $\dfrac{1}{2}$ or 0.5

15. $\dfrac{11}{20}$

16. 17,576,000 different license plates

17. D

18. E

19. C

20. $x = 4.74$

21. Perimeter = 10.54

Practice 81

a. $0.363636\ldots = \dfrac{4}{11}$

b. 840 ways

c. E

d. $a_{103} = 674$

e. $g_6 - g_2 = 38,850$

f. Area = 87.67 square centimeters

Problem Set 81

1. True

2. True

3. A

4. B

5. $6 + \dfrac{9}{2} + \dfrac{27}{8} + \dfrac{81}{32} + \ldots = 24$

6. Sum does not exist

7. $0.1111\ldots = \dfrac{1}{9}$

8. $0.626262\ldots = \dfrac{62}{99}$

9. $\dfrac{1}{7}$

10. $\dfrac{1}{6}$

11. $\dfrac{2}{13}$

12. $\dfrac{3}{5}$ or 0.6

13. 720 ways

14. 15,120 arrangements

15. 60 ways

16. 924 committees

17. 35 different combinations

18. E

19. C

20. $a_{100} = 473$

21. $g_5 - g_2 = 756$

22. Area = 10.63 square centimeters

Practice 82

a. B

b. 6,720 ways

c. $\dfrac{1}{12}$

d. $\dfrac{9}{16}$

e. $x_5 = 4$

Problem Set 82

1. True
2. False
3. D
4. B
5. $18 + 6 + 2 + \dfrac{2}{3} + \ldots = 27$
6. $30 - 6 + \dfrac{6}{5} - \dfrac{6}{25} + \ldots = 25$
7. 120 ways
8. 151,200 arrangements
9. 6,720 ways
10. 24,310 teams
11. 2,002 combinations
12. $d = 4$
13. 45,697,600 different numbers
14. $\dfrac{1}{22}$
15. $\dfrac{1}{3}$
16. $\dfrac{2}{5}$ or 0.4
17. D
18. E
19. B
20. $g_{12} \div g_{16} = \dfrac{1}{16}$
21. $x_4 = -3$

Practice 83

a. $0.434343\ldots = \dfrac{43}{99}$
b. $\dfrac{7}{36}$
c. $\dfrac{3}{14}$
d. Mean = 83.2
e. $n = 5$
f. Average fuel consumption = 31.4 miles per gallon

Problem Set 83

1. False
2. False
3. $0.3333\ldots = \dfrac{1}{3}$
4. $0.151515\ldots = \dfrac{5}{33}$

5. 154,440 arrangements
6. 6,652,800 ways
7. 126 committees
8. 792 combinations
9. 0.00073
10. 11,880 possibilities
11. $\dfrac{1}{4}$ or 0.25
12. $\dfrac{4}{27}$
13. $\dfrac{5}{17}$
14. Mean = 1,100 thousand dollars
15. Median = 1,200 thousand dollars; Mode = 1,400 thousand dollars
16. 82.5
17. C
18. E
19. $\log_a \dfrac{s}{t^2} = -15$
20. 376
21. $n = 3$
22. Gary's average score = 87.4

Practice 84

a. $\dfrac{25}{36}$
b. $\dfrac{83}{168}$
c. Standard deviation = 8,810.11
d. E
e. Mean = 76
f. B

Problem Set 84

1. True
2. True
3. $a_{31} = 213$
4. $r = \dfrac{2}{3}$
5. $a_1 = \dfrac{1}{2}$ or 0.5
6. 40,320 ways
7. 60 ways
8. 0.0005
9. 3,003 combinations
10. $\dfrac{7}{30}$

11. $\dfrac{25}{36}$

12. $\dfrac{28}{153}$

13. $\dfrac{31}{70}$

14. Range = 5,273; Interquartile range = 2,435

15. Standard deviation = 1,582.19

16. D

17. C

18. C

19. Mean = $\dfrac{11}{14}$

20. Average = 84.4

21. Mean = 80

22. E

CHAPTER 13

Practice 85
  a. 180 feet per second
  b. E
  c. C
  d. Standard deviation = 9.24;
      Median = 25
  e. $\lim\limits_{x \to -2} \dfrac{x+8}{x-1} = -2$
  f. At least 4 miles.

Problem Set 85
1. True
2. True
3. $d = -6$
4. $a_{10} = 4{,}374$
5. $a_1 = 4$
6. 48 feet per second
7. 120 feet per second
8. A
9. D
10. 1,287 combinations
11. 36 pizzas
12. 990 possibilities
13. $\dfrac{1}{4}$ or 0.25
14. $\dfrac{23}{42}$
15. 676,000 control codes
16. Mean = 30.67; Range = 48
17. Standard deviation = 13.41;
      Median = 33.50
18. C
19. A
20. $\lim\limits_{x \to -2} (x^2 - 5x + 6) = 20$
21. $\lim\limits_{x \to -1} \dfrac{x+3}{x-1} = -1$
22. At least a 63.

Practice 86
  a. E
  b. Slope = −56
  c. D
  d. $\lim\limits_{x \to -3} \dfrac{x^2 - 9}{x+3} = -6$
  e. Least possible range = 10
  f. 80 feet per second

Problem Set 86
1. True
2. True
3. $r = 6$
4. Sum = 5,550
5. 120 combinations
6. 20,160 different ways
7. 0.49
8. $\dfrac{1}{2}$ or 0.5
9. Mean = 74.8; Range = 48.7
10. Standard deviation: 13.99;
      Median = 73.65
11. D
12. B
13. Slope = 6
14. Slope = −24
15. D
16. B
17. $\lim\limits_{x \to 3} \dfrac{x^2 + 4x - 3}{x^2 - 2x} = 6$
18. $\lim\limits_{x \to -2} \dfrac{x^2 - 4}{x+2} = -4$
19. $g(-8) = 11$
20. Least possible range = 9
21. Average = 50.86 points
22. 30 feet per second

Practice 87
  a. B
  b. E
  c. D
  d. B
  e. $n = 8$
  f. 64 feet

Problem Set 87
1. True
2. True
3. 1,680 arrangements
4. 21 choices
5. $\dfrac{4}{7}$
6. $\dfrac{17}{28}$
7. Mean = 35.4; Range = 36.0
8. Standard deviation = 11.24;
      Median = 35.50

9. Slope = −12
10. Slope = −10
11. A
12. E
13. C
14. D
15. B
16. E
17. C
18. C
19. $k = -3.1$
20. $h(3) = -5$
21. $n = 11$
22. 144 feet

Practice 88

a. Area = 42
b. $\int_{2}^{4} 9x^3\,dx = 540$
c. B
d. $x = 56.3$
e. Sum = 1,120.5
f. Radius = 35.68 meters

Problem Set 88

1. True
2. True
3. $\dfrac{8}{15}$
4. 0.42
5. Mean = 31.7; Range = 48.0
6. Standard deviation = 14.02;
    Median = 27.50
7. C
8. B
9. E
10. A
11. D
12. A
13. Area = 9
14. Area = 28
15. $\int_{0}^{2} 10x\,dx = 20$
16. $\int_{1}^{3} 7x^3\,dx = 140$
17. E
18. A
19. $x = 73.1$
20. $\sqrt[3]{6n} = 7.9$
21. Sum = 788
22. Radius = 56.42 yards

CHAPTER 14

Practice 89
a. $\int_4^8 9x^3\,dx = 8,640$

b. Area $= \dfrac{112}{3}$

c. E
d. D
e. $814.51

Problem Set 89
1. False
2. True
3. $\dfrac{56}{135}$
4. 1,365 teams
5. C
6. E
7. D
8. B
9. $\lim\limits_{x\to 3}(-x^2+8x-3)=12$
10. $\lim\limits_{x\to 0}\dfrac{x^2+4x}{x}=4$
11. $\int_0^5 8x\,dx = 100$
12. $\int_2^6 5x^3\,dx = 1,600$
13. Area = 2
14. Area $= \dfrac{74}{3}$
15. E
16. C
17. E
18. B
19. B
20. Sum = 2,001,000
21. $x = 3,001$
22. $282.36

Practice 90
a. $\dfrac{1}{153}$
b. Weighted mean price = $14.40/item
c. E
d. D
e. $\lim\limits_{x\to 5}\dfrac{x^2-2x-15}{x-5}=8$
f. 3,921,225 combinations

Problem Set 90
1. True
2. True
3. 0.125 or $\dfrac{1}{8}$
4. $\dfrac{1}{91}$
5. $\dfrac{1}{6}$
6. Slope = 3
7. Slope = −6
8. A
9. E
10. Mean = 80.6; Range = 112.0
11. Standard deviation = 29.2; Median = 84.0
12. Weighted mean price = $1.98/lb
13. $\int_0^4 3x^2\,dx = 64$
14. $\int_1^8 10x^{\frac{2}{3}}\,dx = 186$
15. A
16. C
17. D
18. B
19. $x = -\dfrac{5}{2}$
20. $CD = 4.85$
21. $\lim\limits_{x\to 4}\dfrac{x^2-x-12}{x-4}=7$
22. 593,775 combinations

Practice 91
a. $\dfrac{28}{5,995}$
b. E
c. A
d. C
e. B
f. 121 feet

Problem Set 91
1. True
2. False
3. $10-4+1.6-0.64+\ldots = \dfrac{50}{7}$
4. Sum does not exist

5. 336 arrangements

6. 36 combinations

7. $\dfrac{1}{2}$ or 0.5

8. $\dfrac{7}{1,650}$

9. 456,976,000 codes

10. E

11. A

12. D

13. B

14. A

15. C

16. E

17. D

18. B

19. D

20. B

21. C

22. 20 feet

Practice 92

a. B

b. E

c. $a_1 = 79.1$, $\angle A_1 = 87.6°$, $\angle B_1 = 50.4°$,
$a_2 = 11.5$, $\angle A_2 = 8.4°$, $\angle B_2 = 129.6°$

d. B

e. -64

f. 75%

Problem Set 92

1. True

2. False

3. $a_{25} = 4$

4. $g_1 = 8$

5. 0.00051

6. $\dfrac{25}{36}$

7. Area = $\dfrac{56}{3}$

8. Area = 1.4

9. Mean = 2.99; Range = 2.41

10. Standard deviation = 0.72; Median = 3.04

11. D

12. E

13. A

14. C

15. $b = 6.6$, $\angle A = 35.5°$, $\angle C = 104.5°$

16. $c_1 = 44.4$, $\angle C_1 = 58.8°$, $\angle A_1 = 74.2°$,
$c_2 = 23.8$, $\angle C_2 = 27.2°$, $\angle A_2 = 105.8°$

17. $a_1 = 79.3$, $\angle A_1 = 98.7°$, $\angle B_1 = 46.3°$,
$a_2 = 15.7$, $\angle A_2 = 11.3°$, $\angle B_2 = 133.7°$

18. D

19. A

20. $d = -195$

21. -27

22. 78%

Practice 93

a. $\dfrac{16}{35}$

b. D

c. A

d. D

e. B

f. 5.78 minutes

Problem Set 93

1. True

2. True

3. $3.3333... = \dfrac{10}{3}$

4. $0.292929... = \dfrac{29}{99}$

5. $\dfrac{4}{19}$

6. $\dfrac{9}{25}$

7. C

8. E

9. $\lim\limits_{x \to -1}(-x^3 + 5x^2 - 7) = -1$

10. $\lim\limits_{x \to -5} \dfrac{x^2 + 5x}{x^2 + 2x - 15} = \dfrac{5}{8}$

11. D

12. B

13. $c_1 = 52.0$, $\angle C_1 = 90.1°$, $\angle A_1 = 59.9°$,
$c_2 = 25.9$, $\angle C_2 = 29.9°$, $\angle A_2 = 120.1°$

14. $a_1 = 75.9$, $\angle A_1 = 65.1°$, $\angle B_1 = 72.9°$,
$a_2 = 43.0$, $\angle A_2 = 30.9°$, $\angle B_2 = 107.1°$

15. A

16. E

17. C

18. B

19. B

20. D

21. C

22. 1.41 days

Practice 94

a. E

b. B

c. D

d. $m = 1$

e. $n = 9$

f. 10,000

Problem Set 94

1. True

2. True

3. 28 combinations

4. 60 ways

5. C

6. D

7. $\int_0^3 14x\,dx = 63$

8. $\int_1^6 25x^4\,dx = 38{,}875$

9. B

10. D

11. E

12. C

13. B

14. C

15. D

16. A

17. E

18. C

19. D

20. $n = -2$

21. $b = -6$

22. 0.000018

Practice 95

a. E

b. D

c. C

d. B

e. $g_2 - g_1 = 5$

f. 8 miles

Problem Set 95

1. True

2. False

3. 364 combinations

4. 720 arrangements

5. $\dfrac{1}{24}$

6. $\dfrac{4}{7}$

7. C

8. A

9. C

10. E

11. D

12. B

13. C

14. E

15. B

16. B

17. E

18. D

19. $g(f(3)) = 8$

20. $a_2 - a_1 = 3$

21. 2.24

22. 100 pounds

find the answers graphically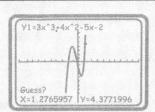

factory costs are a linear function

formula $\{$ 2, 3, ...
$4n - 1$ value ... 23, 27, ...

$\begin{vmatrix} a & b \\ c & d \end{vmatrix} = ad - bc$ $\}$ value

CHAPTER TESTS

just cross multiply and then subtract

$$\cos 2u = \begin{cases} \cos^2 u - \sin^2 u \\ 2\cos^2 u - 1 \\ 1 - 2\sin^2 u \end{cases}$$

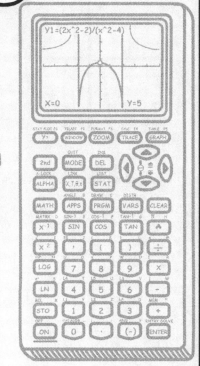

exponential functions

$y = 2^x$

$(-1, 2)$ $(1, 2)$

$(0, 1)$

$y = \left(\frac{1}{2}\right)^x$ or 2^{-x}

reflects across

$x^3 + 2x^2 - 5x - 6 = 0$

$(x-2)(x+3)(x+1) = 0$

Chapter 1 Test

Tell whether each sentence below is true or false.

1. If a vertical line crosses the graph of an equation more than once, then the equation does not represent a
(1) function.

2. A graph with odd symmetry looks the same when you reflect it across the y-axis.
(4)

3. A function created by substituting one function into another is called a composite function.
(6)

Tell whether each graph below represents a function.

4.
(1)
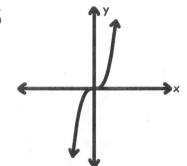

5.
(1)
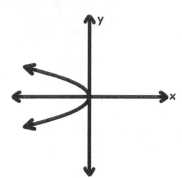

Select the function that represents each graph described below.

6. The graph of $y = 5x^2$ shifted 1 place to the left.
(3)

    A. $y = 5(x+1)^2$ B. $y = 5(x-1)^2$ C. $y = 5x^2 + 1$

    D. $y = 5x^2 - 1$ E. $y = (5x+1)^2$

7. The graph of $y = x^3$ shifted down 2 places and to the right 3 places.
(3)

    A. $y = (x-2)^2 - 3$ B. $y = (x+3)^3 + 2$ C. $y = (x+3)^3 - 3$

    D. $y = (x-3)^3 + 2$ E. $y = (x-3)^3 - 2$

Select the best answer to each question below.

8. Given a function $y = g(x)$, which of the following represents a shift of 2 places to the left?
(3)

    A. $y = g(x) - 2$ B. $y = g(x-2)$ C. $y = g(x+2)$

    D. $y = g(x) + 2$ E. $y = 2g(x)$

9. If $(4,0)$ is a point on the graph of $y = f(x)$, which of the following must be on the graph of $y = -f(x)$?
(4)

    A. $(0,4)$ B. $(-4,0)$ C. $(4,0)$

    D. $(0,-4)$ E. $(4,4)$

Answer each of the following questions using the graphs below.

A.
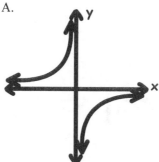

B.
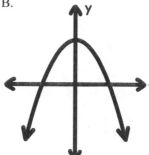

C.
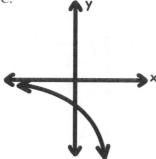

D.
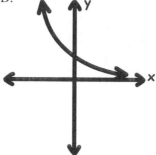

10. Which of the choices above represents the reflection of the graph below across the y-axis?
(4)

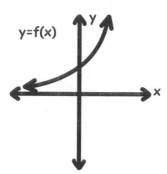

11. Which graph above has symmetry about the origin?
(4)

12. Which graph above has symmetry across the y-axis?
(4)

47

Answer each question below.

13. Which of the choices below represents a vertical compression of the graph below by one-half?
(5)

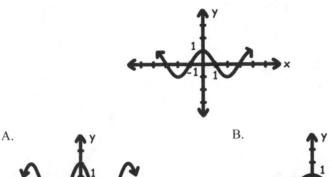

A.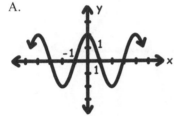

B.

C.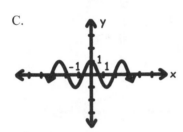

D.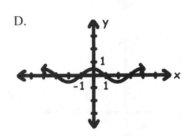

14. Which of the choices below represents a horizontal stretching of the graph below by a factor of 2?
(5)

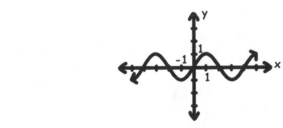

A.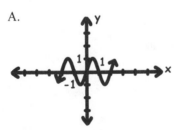

B.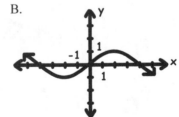

C.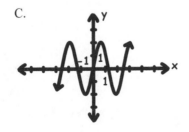

D.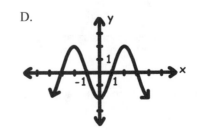

48

Evaluate each function below for the given value.

15. If $f(x) = -2x + 1$ and $x(t) = t - 3$, find $f(x(2))$.
(6)

16. If $f(x) = 4x - 2$ and $x(t) = \sqrt{t+2}$, find $f(x(7))$.
(6)

Select the decomposition of each function below.

17. Which two functions below are a decomposition of $f(x(t)) = 2\sqrt{t^3 - 8}$?
(6)

    A. $f(x) = 2x^3$; $x(t) = \sqrt{t-8}$ B. $f(x) = 2\sqrt{x-8}$; $x(t) = t^3$

    C. $f(x) = 2x$; $x(t) = \sqrt{t^3 - 8}$ D. $f(x) = 2\sqrt{x}$; $x(t) = t - 8$

    E. Either B or C

18. Which two functions below are a decomposition of $u(v(x)) = \dfrac{1}{(x+4)^2}$?
(6)

    A. $u(x) = \dfrac{1}{x^2}$; $v(x) = x + 4$ B. $u(x) = \dfrac{1}{x}$; $v(x) = x + 4$

    C. $u(x) = x + 4$; $v(x) = \dfrac{1}{x^2}$ D. $u(x) = \dfrac{1}{x}$; $v(x) = \dfrac{1}{x+4}$

    E. Either C or D

Find the domain and range of each function below.

19. If $h(x) = \dfrac{1}{2x - 8}$ and $g(x) = -2x$, find the domain and range of $(h \circ g)(x)$.
(6)

    A. Domain: $\{x \mid x \neq -2\}$; Range: All real numbers

    B. Domain: All real numbers except -2; Range: $\{y \mid y \neq 0\}$

    C. Domain: $-\infty < x < \infty$; Range: All real numbers except 0

    D. Domain: All real numbers except 0; Range: All real numbers except -2

    E. Domain: $-\infty < x < \infty$; Range: $-\infty < y < \infty$

20. If $m(x) = \sqrt{x - 4}$ and $n(x) = x + 1$, find the domain and range of $(m \circ n)(x)$.
(6)

    A. Domain: $-\infty < x < \infty$; Range: $-\infty < y < \infty$

    B. Domain: $3 \leq x < \infty$; Range: $-\infty < y < \infty$

    C. Domain: $-\infty < x < \infty$; Range: All real positive numbers

    D. Domain: $\{x \mid x \geq 3\}$; Range: All real positive numbers and zero

    E. Domain: $\{x \mid x \neq 3\}$; Range: All real numbers

Each top graph below is a one-to-one function. (Hint: a one-to-one function is just a function whose inverse is also a function.) Select the choice that best matches the graph of its inverse function.

21.
(7)

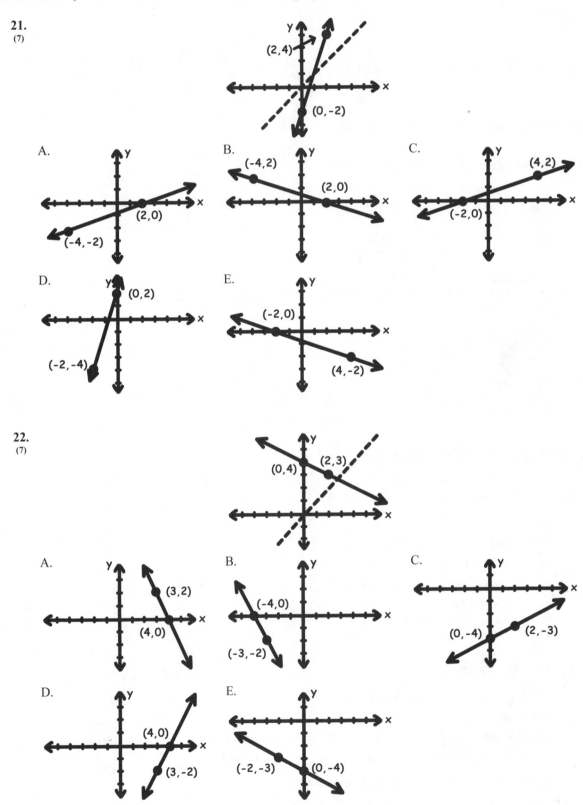

Graph each function below by using transformations. Select the choice that best matches your graph.

23. $f(x) = 3(x+2)^2 - 3$
(5)

A.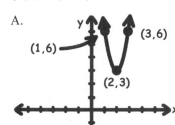

B.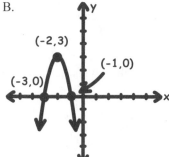

C.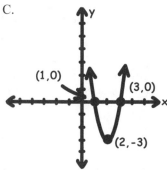

D.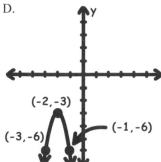

E.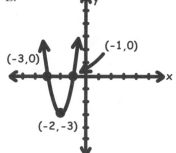

24. $g(x) = -\dfrac{1}{2}(x-1)^2 + 2$
(5)

A.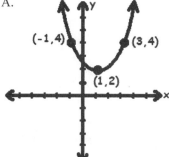

B.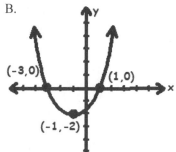

C.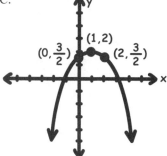

D.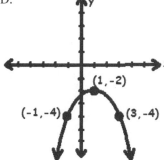

E.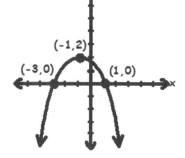

Chapter 2 Test

Tell whether each sentence below is true or false.

1. The graph of every quadratic function is a parabola.
(9)

2. If any number k is a solution to a polynomial equation, then that polynomial must factor into the form
(9) $(x+k)$ (some expression).

Select the equation that represents each line below.

3. A line with a slope of -3 that passes through the point $(-7,0)$.
(8)

    A. $y-2=-3(x-7)$ B. $y-0=-3(x+7)$ C. $y=-3x-7$

    D. $y=21x$ E. $-3x+y-7=0$

4. A line with a slope of $\dfrac{3}{4}$ and that passes through the point $(0,4)$.
(8)

    A. $y=\dfrac{3}{4}x-4$ B. $y-0=\dfrac{3}{4}(x-4)$ C. $y+\dfrac{3}{4}x-4=0$

    D. $y=\dfrac{3}{4}(x-0)$ E. $y-4=\dfrac{3}{4}(x-0)$

Select the vertex form of each quadratic function below.

5. $f(x)=-2x^2-16x-33$
(10)

    A. $f(x)=-2(x+4)^2-49$ B. $f(x)=-(2x+4)^2-17$ C. $f(x)=-2(x+4)^2-1$

    D. $f(x)=-2(x-2)^2-31$ E. $f(x)=-2(x-4)^2+1$

6. $g(x)=3x^2-18x+29$
(10)

    A. $g(x)=3(x+3)^2-2$ B. $g(x)=3(x-3)^2+20$ C. $g(x)=(3x+3)^2+26$

    D. $g(x)=3(x-3)^2+2$ E. $g(x)=-3(x-3)^2+56$

Select the function for each parabola below.

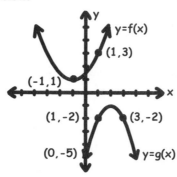

7. $y = f(x)$
(10)

    A. $y = \dfrac{1}{2}(x+1)^2 + 1$ B. $y = -2(x-3)^2 + 1$ C. $y = x^2 - 3x + 1$

    D. $y = 2(x-1)^2 + 3$ E. $y = \dfrac{1}{2}(x-1)^2 - 1$

8. $y = g(x)$
(10)

    A. $y = -(x-1)^2 - 2$ B. $y = 2x^2 - 5x$ C. $y = -(x-3)^2 - 2$

    D. $y = -x^2 + 2x + 3$ E. $y = -x^2 + 4x - 5$

Tell the maximum number of turning points that the graph of each polynomial below can have.

9. $m(x) = 8x^3 - 2x^2 + 4x$ **10.** $n(x) = 3x^4 - 6x^3 - 7x^2$
(12)   (12)

Answer each question below.

11. The graph of $y = f(x)$ is shown in the figure below. Which of the following could be $f(x)$?
(12)

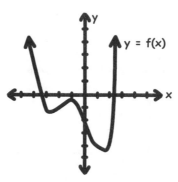

    A. a B. $ax + b$ C. $ax^2 + bx + c$

    D. $ax^3 + bx^2 + cx + d$ E. $ax^4 + bx^3 + cx^2 + dx + e$

12. If -6 and 3 are both zeros of the polynomial $g(x)$, then which of the following is a factor of $g(x)$?
(15)

    A. $x^2 + 18$ B. $x^2 - 3x - 18$ C. $x^2 - 9x + 18$

    D. $x^2 + 3x - 18$ E. $x^2 - 18$

Use the Remainder Theorem to find each remainder below.

13. What is the remainder when dividing $g(x) = 4x^4 - 14x^3 + 7x^2 - 5x + 7$ by $x - 3$?
(13)

14. What is the remainder when dividing $f(x) = -3x^3 - 8x^2 + x + 7$ by $x + 2$?
(13)

Do each division problem below with polynomial division. Select the choice that matches your answer.

15. $\dfrac{-2x^3 + 11x^2 - 8x + 15}{-x + 5}$
(13)

A. $(2x^2 - 21x + 113) - \dfrac{550}{-x + 5}$

B. $(2x^2 - x - 3) + \dfrac{30}{-x + 5}$

C. $2x^2 - x + 3$

D. $2x^2 + x + 3$

E. $(-2x - 3) + \dfrac{30}{-x + 5}$

16. $3x + 2 \overline{)6x^3 - 2x^2 + 8x + 3}$
(13)

A. $(2x^2 + 2x + 3) - \dfrac{3}{3x + 2}$

B. $(2x^2 - 2x + 4) + \dfrac{-5}{3x + 2}$

C. $(2x + 4) - \dfrac{5}{3x + 2}$

D. $2x^2 - 2x + 4$

E. $(2x^2 - 2x - 4) + \dfrac{11}{3x + 2}$

Use a graphing calculator to find the stated zero (x-intercept) and local maximum or minimum of each function below. Round any irrational answers to two decimal places.

17. For the function, $g(x) = 2x^4 - x^3 - 9x^2 + 4x + 4$, find the largest zero and the local maximum.
(16)

18. For the function, $h(x) = 2x^3 - 3x^2 - 5x + 6$, find the smallest zero and the local minimum.
(16)

Find the polynomial function for each set of zeros below. Assume a stretch factor of $a = 1$. Select the choice that matches your answer.

19. 2, $-1 - \sqrt{7}i$, $-1 + \sqrt{7}i$
(15)

A. $y = x^2 + 2x + 8$

B. $y = x^3 + 6x^2 - 14x - 4$

C. $y = x^3 + 3x^2 - 4x + 14$

D. $y = x^3 + 7x - 12$

E. $y = x^3 + 4x - 16$

20. -3, 1, $2 - \sqrt{5}i$, $2 + \sqrt{5}i$
(15)

A. $y = x^4 - 2x^3 - 2x^2 + 30x - 27$

B. $y = x^2 + 2x + 9$

C. $y = x^3 - 4x^2 + 2x - 15$

D. $y = x^4 - 2x^2 - 21x + 10$

E. $y = x^4 + 4x^3 + 2x^2 - 24x - 27$

Find the zeros of each polynomial below. List any zeros of multiplicity as many times as they appear. (Hint: On problem 22 one of the zeros is 1.)

21. $f(x) = x(x+4)^3(x-6)^4$
(14)

22. $g(x) = 6x^3 - 5x^2 - 3x + 2$
(13)

Graph the quadratic function below (without a calculator). Select the choice that best matches your graph.

23. $f(x) = -(x+3)^2 + 1$
(10)

A.
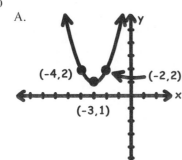

B.
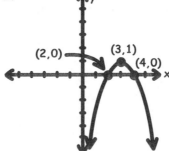

C.
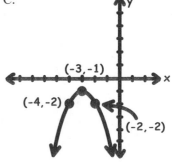

D.
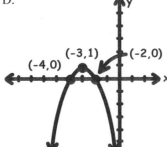

E.
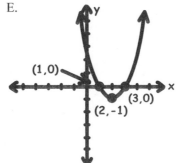

Solve the word problem below.

24. Over the weekend, Alexander and his dad went to a driving range to hit golf balls. If the path of the ball
(9) Alexander hit can be represented by the function $y(x) = -x^2 + 30x$, where x is the horizontal distance and y is the height (both in feet), how far from Alex did the ball land?

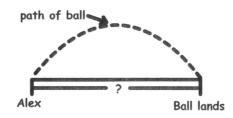

Chapter 3 Test

Tell whether each sentence below is true or false.

1. To find the vertical asymptotes of a rational function, figure out what values for x make the denominator
(17) equal 0.

2. For a rational function, when the degree of the denominator is higher than the degree of the numerator, the
(18) asymptote is always the x-axis (the line $y = 0$).

Do each division problem below with polynomial division. Select the choice that matches your answer.

3. $\dfrac{-5x^3 + 21x^2 - 25x + 21}{-x + 3}$
(13)

A. $(5x^2 - 36x + 133) + \dfrac{420}{-x + 3}$ 　　B. $5x^2 - 6x + 7$ 　　C. $(-5x - 7) + \dfrac{-x + 3}{42}$

D. $-5x^2 - 6x - 7$ 　　E. $(5x^2 - 6x - 7) + \dfrac{42}{-x + 3}$

4. $3x - 2 \overline{)-6x^4 + x^3 + 14x^2 - 23x + 11}$
(13)

A. $(-2x^3 - x^2 + 4x - 5) + \dfrac{1}{3x - 2}$ 　　B. $(-2x^3 - x^2 + 4x + 5) + \dfrac{21}{3x - 2}$

C. $(-2x^3 + 5x^2 + 4x + 5) + \dfrac{21}{3x - 2}$ 　　D. $(-2x^2 - 4x - 5) + \dfrac{1}{3x - 2}$

E. $-2x^3 - x^2 + 4x - 5$

Find the vertical asymptotes of each rational function below.

5. $f(x) = \dfrac{x - 1}{3x + 2}$ 　　　　　　　　**6.** $g(x) = \dfrac{-5x}{x^2 - x - 6}$
(17) 　　　　　　　　　　　　　　　　(17)

Find the horizontal or slant asymptotes of each rational function below.

7. $f(x) = \dfrac{x^2}{(x + 1)^3}$ 　　　　　　　**8.** $g(x) = \dfrac{-3x + 1}{x - 5}$
(18) 　　　　　　　　　　　　　　　　(18)

9. $h(x) = \dfrac{2x^2 - x - 2}{2x + 3}$
(18)

A. $y = x + 1$ 　　B. $y = 2x - 1$ 　　C. $y = -x - 2$

D. $y = 2x^2 + x + 1$ 　　E. $y = x - 2$

56

Answer each question below.

10. f is a function. Suppose the following two statements are true of f.
(18)

      I. f has a root at $x = -1$.

      II. The graph of $y = f(x)$ has exactly two asymptotes at $x = 4$ and $y = 2$.

Which of the following functions could be f?

    A. $f(x) = (x+1)(x-2)$ B. $f(x) = \dfrac{3x-3}{x-2}$ C. $f(x) = \dfrac{2x+2}{x-4}$

    D. $f(x) = (x-4)(x+1)$ E. $f(x) = \dfrac{(x-4)(x-2)}{(x+1)}$

11. If $f(x) = 4x - 3$ and $f^{-1}(g(3)) = 2$, which of the following could be $g(x)$?
(7)

    A. $g(x) = 4x$ B. $g(x) = \dfrac{-x+2}{x-3}$ C. $g(x) = x^2 - 3$

    D. $g(x) = \dfrac{2x-1}{x-2}$ E. $g(x) = -3x + 7$

12. Select the rational function that represents the graph to the right.
(21)

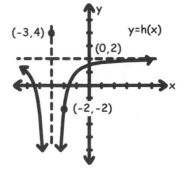

    A. $h(x) = \dfrac{1}{x+3} + 3$ B. $h(x) = \dfrac{-4}{(x+3)^2} + 2$

    C. $h(x) = \dfrac{-4}{x-3}$ D. $h(x) = \dfrac{1}{(x+3)^2} - 1$

    E. $h(x) = \dfrac{-1}{(x+3)^2} + 2$

13. Use a graphing calculator to graph the rational function $y = \dfrac{x+7}{x^2-4}$. Show the equation on the screen by
(19)

pressing $\boxed{\text{TRACE}}$ after you're finished. Select the choice that best matches your graph.

A.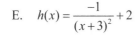

    A. 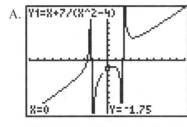   B. 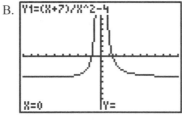   C. 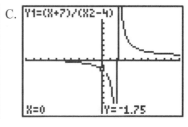

    D. 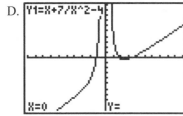   E. 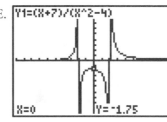

Select whether the graph of each function below has even symmetry (across the y-axis), odd symmetry (across the origin), or neither.

14. $y = 1 - \dfrac{1}{3x^4}$
(4)

    A. even symmetry   B. odd symmetry   C. neither

15. $y = \dfrac{x^2 - 1}{4x^3}$
(19)

    A. even symmetry   B. odd symmetry   C. neither

16. $y = \dfrac{x^3 - 2}{3 + x}$
(19)

    A. even symmetry   B. odd symmetry   C. neither

Factor each expression below. Select the choice that matches your answer.

17. $x^3 - y^3$
(20)
    A. $(x+y)(x-y)$ B. $(x-y)(x^2 - xy + y^2)$ C. $(x-y)^3$
    D. $(x-y)^2$ E. $(x-y)(x^2 + xy + y^2)$

18. $x^3 + 8$
(20)
    A. $(x+2)^2$ B. $(x+2)(x^2 - 2x + 4)$ C. $(x+2)(x^2 + 2x + 4)$
    D. $(x+2)(x-2)$ E. $(x+2)^3$

19. $a^3 + 3a^2 b + 3ab^2 + b^3$
(20)
    A. $(a+b)(a-b)$ B. $(a-b)(a^2 + ab + b^2)$ C. $(a+b)^2$
    D. $(a+b)^3$ E. $(a+b)(a^2 - ab + b^2)$

Find the zeros of each polynomial below. List any zeros of multiplicity as many times as they appear. (Hint: On problem 21, one of the zeros is −2.)

20. $f(x) = (x+4)(x-1)^2 (2x+3)^4$ **21.** $g(x) = x^3 + 2x^2 - 7x - 14$
(14)   (14)

Find the matching *x*-value(s) for each function below using a graphing calculator. (Hint: On problem 23, adjust the range of *x* and *y*-values to Xmin = –10, Xmax = 10, Ymin = –50, Ymax = 50.)

22.
(22)
$$y = \frac{-6x^2 - 15x - 15}{3x^2 + 4x - 1}, \ y = -3, \ x = ?$$

23.
(22)
$$y = 2x^3 - 7x^2 - 5x + 9, \ y = 5, \ x = ?$$

Solve the word problem below.

24.
(17)
Kappa Corporation owns a factory that makes PVC pipe. The cost (*C*) to run the factory each year can be represented by the function $C(p) = 3p + 300,000$ where *p* is the number of pounds of PVC pipe produced.

Use this to write another function to determine the cost per pound if the factory produces *p* pounds. Using this new function, what would be the cost per pound if the factory produced 16,000 pounds in a year? Round your answer to the nearest cent.

Chapter 4 Test

Tell whether each sentence below is true or false.

1. An exponential decay function has a negative growth rate.
(24)

2. The graph of $y = \log x$ rises faster and faster as x approaches infinity.
(27)

Find each logarithm below without using a calculator.

3. $\log_3 3^6$
(26)

4. $10^{\log 9}$
(26)

Calculate the value of each function below. Estimate any irrational answers to 2 decimal places.

5. If $y(x) = \ln(4x)$, then $y(2) = ?$
(30)

6. If $y(x) = 750e^{0.16x}$, then $y(3) = ?$
(29)

Solve each exponential equation below by setting the exponents equal to each other.

7. $4^{3x+5} = 64$
(25)

8. $\left(\dfrac{1}{3}\right)^{6-x} = 81$
(25)

Use the change of base formula to find each log below. Estimate your answers to four decimal places.

9. $\log_7 5$
(26)

10. $\log_4 15$
(26)

Select the domain and range of each exponential function below.

11. $y = 3^{4-x} - 5$
(23)

    A. Domain: $x \geq 0$; Range: $y \geq 0$ B. Domain: $(-\infty,\ 4]$; Range: $[0,\ +\infty)$

    C. Domain: $(-\infty,\ +\infty)$; Range: $(-\infty,\ +\infty)$ D. Domain: $(-\infty,\ +\infty)$; Range: $(-5,\ +\infty)$

    E. Domain: $[4,\ +\infty)$; Range: $[-5,\ +\infty)$

12. $y = \log(2x - 4)$
(26)

    A. Domain: $[2,\ +\infty)$; Range: $(-\infty,\ +\infty)$ B. Domain: $(-\infty,\ 2]$; Range: $[0,\ +\infty)$

    C. Domain: $x \geq 2$; Range: $y \geq 0$ D. Domain: $(-\infty,\ +\infty)$; Range: $(-\infty,\ +\infty)$

    E. Domain: $(2,\ +\infty)$; Range: $(-\infty,\ +\infty)$

Answer the question below.

13. Solve the log equation $5\log x^2 = 7$ by graphing on a calculator. Estimate your answer to two decimal
(28) places.

Rewrite each expression below as a single log. Select the choice that best matches your answer.

14. $\log_4(x-3) + \log_4(x+3)$
(28)

    A. $\log_4(2x)$ B. $-\log_4 6$ C. $\log_4(x^2 - 9)$

    D. $\log_{x-3}(x+3)$ E. $\log_4\left(\dfrac{x-3}{x+3}\right)$

15. $\ln(2x-12) - \ln(x-6)$
(30)

    A. $\ln(2x^2 - 24x + 72)$ B. $\ln 2$ C. $\ln\left(\dfrac{1}{2}\right)$

    D. $\ln(x-6)$ E. $\ln(3x-18)$

16. $3\log_3 4x$
(28)

    A. $\log_3(4x+3)$ B. $\log_3(12x)$ C. $\log_9 4x$

    D. $\log_3\left(\dfrac{4x}{3}\right)$ E. $\log_3(64x^3)$

Solve each log equation below.

17. $\log_3(5x+1) = 4$ **18.** $\ln(x) + \ln(x-2) = \ln 8$
(28)   (30)

Select the graph for each function below.

19. $y = 3^{x-1} + 1$
(23)

A. 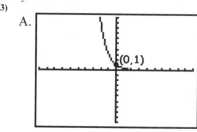   B. 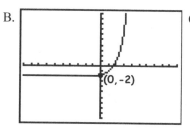   C.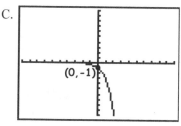

D. 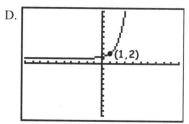   E.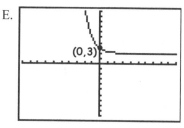

20. $y = -e^{-3x}$
(29)

A.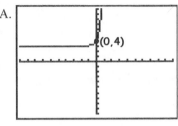

B.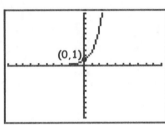

C.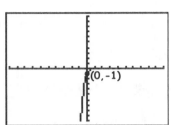

D.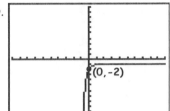

E.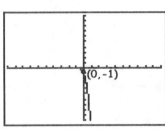

21. $y = \ln(-x) + 2$
(30)

A.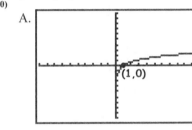

B.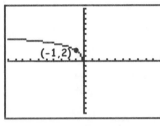

C.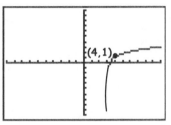

D.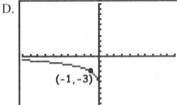

E.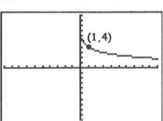

Answer each question below.

22. We deposit $3,200 in a bank that is paying 4% interest once a year. Select a function for P representing the
(29) amount of money we'll have after t years.

    A. $P = 3,200e^{0.04t}$ B. $P = 3,200(0.04)^t$ C. $P = 3,200(1.04)^t$

    D. $P = 3,200(1.0033)^t$ E. $P = 1.04^t$

23. We deposit $700 in a bank that is paying 8% interest continuously. Select a function for P representing the
(29) amount of money we'll have after t years.

    A. $P = 700e^{1.08t}$ B. $P = 700(0.08)^t$ C. $P = 1.08^t$

    D. $P = 700(1.08)^t$ E. $P = 700e^{0.08t}$

Solve the word problem below.

24. A nighttime cough syrup exponentially decays in the bloodstream, as represented by the function
$A(t) = I(0.60)^t$ where t is time in hours and I is the initial amount taken. If Belinda initially took 5 milligrams of the syrup before bed, how much is in her bloodstream when she wakes up, 8 hours later? Round your answer to four decimal places.

Chapter 5 Test

Tell whether each sentence below is true or false.

1. When solving radical equations with square roots, you should always check your answers.
(31)

2. An absolute value function is equal to x when the independent variable is positive or 0, but equal to $-x$
(36) when the independent variable is less than zero.

Write each of the following functions as power functions in the form $y = ax^n$. Select the choice that matches your answer.

3. $y = 4x\sqrt[3]{x^2}$
(32)

    A. $y = 4x^{\frac{3}{5}}$ B. $y = 4x^{\frac{2}{3}}$ C. $y = 4x^{\frac{5}{3}}$

    D. $y = 4x^2$ E. $y = 4x^{\frac{3}{2}}$

4. $y = \dfrac{6}{\sqrt{x^7}}$
(32)

    A. $y = 6x^{-\frac{7}{2}}$ B. $y = 6x^{-7}$ C. $y = 6x^{\frac{1}{7}}$

    D. $y = 6x^{\frac{7}{2}}$ E. $y = 6x^{-\frac{2}{7}}$

Select the inverse of each function below.

5. $f(x) = x^{\frac{1}{4}}$
(33)

    A. $f^{-1}(x) = \log_4 x$ B. $f^{-1}(x) = 4x$ C. $f^{-1}(x) = x^{-4}$

    D. $f^{-1}(x) = x^4$ E. $f^{-1}(x) = \log_{\frac{1}{4}} x$

6. $f(x) = \dfrac{1}{8}x^3$
(33)

    A. $f^{-1}(x) = \dfrac{1}{2}x^{\frac{1}{3}}$ B. $f^{-1}(x) = 2x^{\frac{1}{3}}$ C. $f^{-1}(x) = 4\log_3 x$

    D. $f^{-1}(x) = \log_{\frac{1}{2}} x$ E. $f^{-1}(x) = \log_{\frac{1}{3}}(2x)$

Calculate the correct matching value for each function below.

7. For $f(x) = \begin{cases} -3x^2 + 2, & x < -1 \\ x + 7, & x \geq -1 \end{cases}$ and $x = -2$, find y.
(35)

8. For $f(x) = 3|2x - 5|$ and $x = 1$, find y.
(36)

Select the correct key stroke sequence that should be used to graph each function on the calculator screen.

9. $y = 5|7 - x|$
(36)

A. $\boxed{Y=}$ $\boxed{5}$ $\boxed{MATH}$ $\boxed{\triangleright}$ $\boxed{1}$ $\boxed{7}$ $\boxed{-}$ $\boxed{X,T,\theta,n}$ $\boxed{)}$ $\boxed{GRAPH}$

B. $\boxed{Y=}$ $\boxed{5}$ $\boxed{MATH}$ $\boxed{\triangleleft}$ $\boxed{1}$ $\boxed{7}$ $\boxed{(-)}$ $\boxed{X,T,\theta,n}$ $\boxed{)}$ $\boxed{GRAPH}$

C. $\boxed{Y=}$ $\boxed{5}$ $\boxed{MATH}$ $\boxed{1}$ $\boxed{7}$ $\boxed{-}$ $\boxed{X,T,\theta,n}$ $\boxed{)}$ $\boxed{GRAPH}$

D. $\boxed{Y=}$ $\boxed{5}$ $\boxed{MATH}$ $\boxed{\triangleright}$ $\boxed{3}$ $\boxed{7}$ $\boxed{-}$ $\boxed{X,T,\theta,n}$ $\boxed{)}$ $\boxed{GRAPH}$

E. $\boxed{Y=}$ $\boxed{5}$ $\boxed{MATH}$ $\boxed{\triangleleft}$ $\boxed{X,T,\theta,n}$ $\boxed{(-)}$ $\boxed{7}$ $\boxed{)}$ $\boxed{GRAPH}$

10. $y = \text{int}(0.5x)$
(36)

A. $\boxed{Y=}$ $\boxed{MATH}$ $\boxed{\triangleright}$ $\boxed{3}$ $\boxed{5}$ $\boxed{X,T,\theta,n}$ $\boxed{)}$ $\boxed{MODE}$ $\boxed{\triangledown}$ $\boxed{\triangledown}$ $\boxed{\triangledown}$ $\boxed{\triangledown}$ $\boxed{\triangleright}$ $\boxed{ENTER}$ $\boxed{GRAPH}$

B. $\boxed{Y=}$ $\boxed{MATH}$ $\boxed{5}$ $\boxed{\wedge}$ $\boxed{5}$ $\boxed{X,T,\theta,n}$ $\boxed{)}$ $\boxed{MATH}$ $\boxed{\triangle}$ $\boxed{\triangle}$ $\boxed{\triangle}$ $\boxed{\triangle}$ $\boxed{\triangleright}$ $\boxed{ENTER}$ $\boxed{GRAPH}$

C. $\boxed{Y=}$ $\boxed{MATH}$ $\boxed{\triangleright}$ $\boxed{5}$ $\boxed{.}$ $\boxed{5}$ $\boxed{X,T,\theta,n}$ $\boxed{)}$ $\boxed{MODE}$ $\boxed{\triangledown}$ $\boxed{\triangledown}$ $\boxed{\triangledown}$ $\boxed{\triangledown}$ $\boxed{\triangleright}$ $\boxed{ENTER}$ $\boxed{GRAPH}$

D. $\boxed{Y=}$ $\boxed{MATH}$ $\boxed{\triangleleft}$ $\boxed{5}$ $\boxed{.}$ $\boxed{5}$ $\boxed{X,T,\theta,n}$ $\boxed{)}$ $\boxed{\triangle}$ $\boxed{\triangle}$ $\boxed{\triangle}$ $\boxed{\triangle}$ $\boxed{\triangle}$ $\boxed{ENTER}$ $\boxed{GRAPH}$

E. $\boxed{Y=}$ $\boxed{\triangleright}$ $\boxed{5}$ $\boxed{.}$ $\boxed{5}$ $\boxed{X,T,\theta,n}$ $\boxed{)}$ $\boxed{MODE}$ $\boxed{\triangledown}$ $\boxed{\triangledown}$ $\boxed{\triangledown}$ $\boxed{\triangledown}$ $\boxed{\triangleleft}$ $\boxed{ENTER}$ $\boxed{GRAPH}$

Solve each equation below.

11. $\log\left(\dfrac{x}{10}\right) = -2 + 2\log x$
(28)

12. $\sqrt{3x + 6} - x - 2 = 0$
(31)

13. $\sqrt{t + 7} - \sqrt{t} = 1$
(31)

14. $\dfrac{x^{\frac{1}{4}} - 1}{2} = 4$
(33)

15. $4|x - 5| = 12$
(36)

16. $-|3x + 6| + 8 = 2$
(36)

Answer each question below.

17. If $x = \log_4 t$ and $y = t^3$, what is y in terms of x?
(27)

   A. 3 B. 4^{3x} C. 4^x

   D. x E. $\log_3 x$

18. If $f(x) = 10^x$, then $f^{-1}(x^5) = ?$
(27)

   A. x^5 B. $10x^5$ C. $\ln x^5$

   D. $5\log x$ E. $\log_x 10x^5$

19. What is the range of $f(x) = x^4 - \sqrt{-x-2}$?
(31)

    A. All real numbers less than or equal to -16

    B. All real numbers less than or equal to -14

    C. All real numbers greater than or equal to -14

    D. All real numbers greater than or equal to 16

    E. All real numbers less than or equal to 16

Select the graph for each function below.

20. $y = 4x^{-3}$
(32)

A.
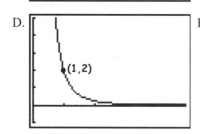

B.
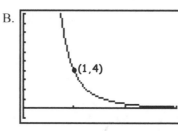

C.
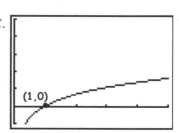

D.
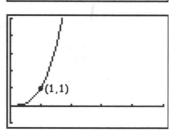

E.
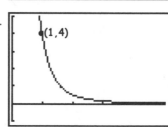

21. $f(x) = \dfrac{1}{2}x^{\frac{4}{3}}$
(32)

A.
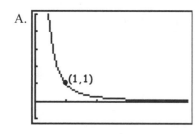

B.
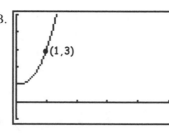

C.
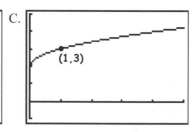

D.
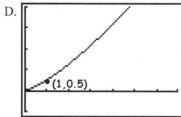

E.

22.
(35)
$$g(x) = \begin{cases} -3x+1, & x < 2 \\ x-4, & x \geq 2 \end{cases}$$

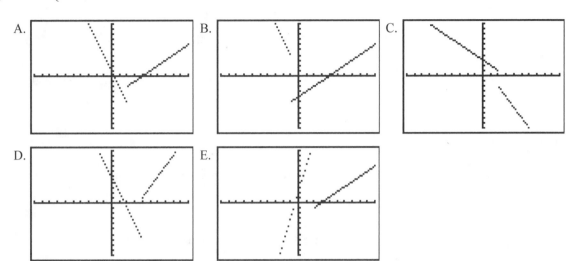

A.   B.   C.

D.   E.

Solve the following word problems.

23. A movie theater is reordering popcorn buckets for the concession stand. The cost for b buckets decreases if
(35) they are purchased in bulk. Additionally, the movie theater gets a $2.00 discount on shipping for every 250 buckets they order. The cost for ordering b buckets can be represented by the function

$$f(x) = \begin{cases} 0.10b+10.00, & b < 250 \\ 0.08b+8.00, & 250 \leq b < 500 \\ 0.05b+6.00, & 500 \leq b < 750 \end{cases}$$. Based on this function, how much would it cost to order 375

buckets?

24. The speed (in feet per second) of a ball tossed up in the air can be represented by the function
(36) $v(t) = 32|t| + 5$ where t is time in seconds. Based on this function, at what time would the speed of the ball be equal to 69 feet per second?

Chapter 6 Test

Tell whether each sentence below is true or false.

1. Using the Law of Cosines, it is possible to find parts of non-right triangles.
(40)

2. The Law of Sines is usually the best rule to use when given two angles and one side of a triangle.
(41)

Answer the question below.

3. Convert the angle measurement $32°54'$ so that the minutes are in decimal form.
(38)

Find each missing angle below for $0° \leq$ angle $\leq 90°$. Don't use a calculator.

4. $\sin \theta = \dfrac{\sqrt{2}}{2}$
(39)

5. $\tan \alpha = \sqrt{3}$
(39)

6. $\cos \theta = \dfrac{1}{2}$
(39)

Find each missing angle below. Estimate your answers to one decimal place.

7.
(39)

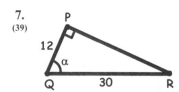

8.
(39)

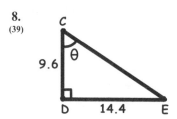

Solve each right triangle below by finding all of its missing parts. Estimate your answers to one decimal place.

9.
(39)

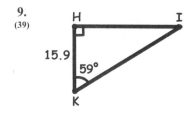

10.
(39)

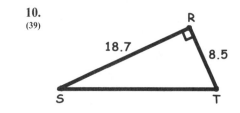

Solve each word problem below. Hint: Draw a picture of each right triangle.

11. In a $58° - 32°$ right triangle, the side adjacent to the $32°$ angle is 41.74 inches. If $\tan 58° = 1.6003$, find
(37) the length of the side opposite the $32°$ angle. Estimate your answer to 3 decimal places.

12. In a $60° - 30°$ right triangle, the length of the side opposite the $30°$ angle is 96.5 meters long. Find the
(39) length of the hypotenuse.

Use the Law of Cosines to find the missing side of each triangle below. Estimate your answers to one decimal place.

13.
(40)

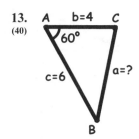

14.
(40)

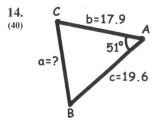

Use the Law of Cosines to find the missing angle of each triangle below. Estimate your answers to one decimal place.

15.
(40)

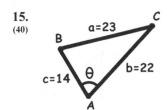

16.
(40)

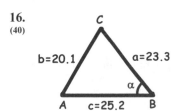

Use the Law of Sines to find the missing side of each triangle below. Estimate your answers to one decimal place.

17.
(41)

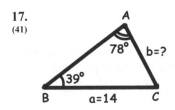

18.
(41)

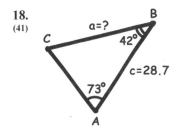

Use the Law of Sines to find the missing angle of each triangle below. Estimate your answers to one decimal place.

19.
(41)

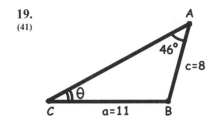

20.
(41)

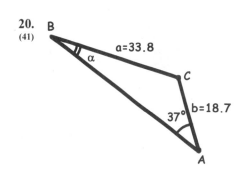

Answer each question below.

21. In the figure to the right, what is $\dfrac{x-z}{y}$ in terms of θ?
(38)

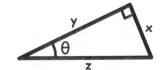

    A. $\cos\theta - \sin\theta$ B. $\tan\theta - \csc\theta$

    C.   1   D. $\tan\theta - \sec\theta$

    E. $\csc\theta - \sec\theta$

22. In the figure to the right, if $\alpha = 58°$, what is the area of the triangle rounded to
(38)
     two decimal places? (Hint: Area of a triangle $= \dfrac{1}{2} \times \text{Base} \times \text{Height}$.)

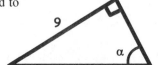

    A.   25.31   B.   47.76

    C.   50.61   D.   64.81

    E.   76.43

23. In the figure to the right, if $\sin\alpha = 0.52$, then what is the value of $\dfrac{x}{z}$? Round
(39)
     your answer to two decimal places.

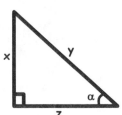

    A. -0.86 B.   0.48

    C.   0.61   D.   0.86

    E.   1.65

Solve the word problem below.

24. Jack, John, and Josh all went camping together, but each one took a separate tent. The paths between the
(37)
     tents form the sides of a right triangle. If Jack's tent is 20 feet from Josh's and the angle formed at Jack's
     tent is $20°$, how far is Josh's tent from John's? Round your answer to two decimal places.

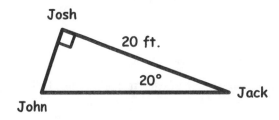

Chapter 7 Test

Tell whether each sentence below is true or false.

1. The period is the change in x that has to occur for the function to run through a complete cycle.
(45)

2. The inverse of the cosine function is $y = \cos^{-1} x$ where x represents some cosine ratio and y represents the
(49) angle ($0 \le x \le \pi$) that goes with it.

Select the matching value for y in each function below.

3. $y = \sin(-240°)$
(43)

     A. $-\dfrac{1}{2}$ B. $-\dfrac{\sqrt{3}}{2}$ C. $\dfrac{1}{2}$ D. $-\dfrac{1}{\sqrt{2}}$ E. $\dfrac{\sqrt{3}}{2}$

4. $y = \tan 45°$
(39)

     A. $\dfrac{1}{\sqrt{2}}$ B. $-\dfrac{1}{\sqrt{2}}$ C. 1 D. -1 E. $\dfrac{\sqrt{3}}{2}$

Find the matching value for y in each function below to 2 decimal places. The independent variable is in radians.

5. $y = \sin \dfrac{\pi}{8}$
(44)

6. $y = \cos\left(-\dfrac{5\pi}{7}\right)$
(44)

Select the correct graph for each function below.

7. $y = \tan 2x$
(46)

A. 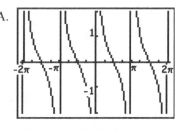   B. 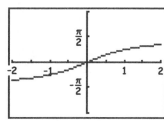   C.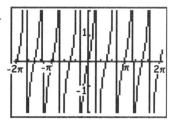

D.   E.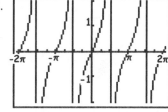

8. $y = e^{-0.2x} \sin 2x$
(48)

A.
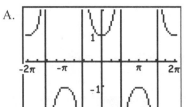

B.
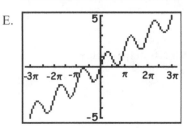

C.
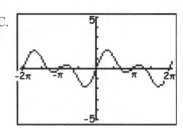

D.
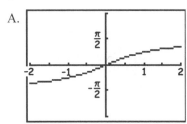

E.
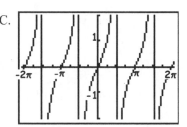

9. $y = \sin^{-1} x$
(49)

A.

B.

C.

D.

E.
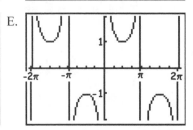

Select the function that represents each graph below.

10.
(46)
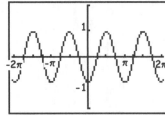

A. $y = \cos 2x$ B. $y = -\cos x$

C. $y = \sin\left(x - \dfrac{\pi}{4}\right)$ D. $y = \sin 2x$

E. $y = -\cos 2x$

11.
(46)

A. $y = \cos\left(x - \dfrac{\pi}{3}\right)$ B. $y = 2\sin\left(x - \dfrac{\pi}{3}\right)$

C. $y = -2\cos(2x)$ D. $y = 2\sin\left(x + \dfrac{\pi}{3}\right)$

E. $y = 2\sin\dfrac{1}{2}x$

Select the answer for each question below.

12. The oscillation of tides in Laguna Beach, California can be modeled with a sinusoidal function. The
(46) difference between the highest and lowest point is 7.4 feet and the period is 12.8 hours. Select the function below that represents the position D of the tides over time t.

A. $D = 7.4\cos\dfrac{\pi}{6.4}t$

B. $D = 3.7\cos\dfrac{1}{6.4}t$

C. $D = 3.7\cos\dfrac{\pi}{6.4}t$

D. $D = 3.7\cos 25.6\pi t$

E. $D = 7.4\cos\dfrac{\pi}{12.8}t$

13. A buoy floats on the water bobbing up and down. The distance between its highest and lowest point is 11
(46) centimeters. The buoy is at its maximum height at $t = 0$ and moves down to its lowest point and back every 4 seconds. Select the function below that represents the position D of the buoy in relationship to the equilibrium point over time t.

A. $D = 11\sin 8\pi t$

B. $D = 11\sin\dfrac{\pi}{2}(t+1)$

C. $D = 5.5\sin\dfrac{\pi}{8}t$

D. $D = 5.5\sin\dfrac{\pi}{2}(t-1)$

E. $D = 5.5\sin\dfrac{\pi}{2}(t+1)$

Select whether each function below has even symmetry, odd symmetry, or neither.

14. $y = \tan 3x$
(47)

A. even symmetry

B. odd symmetry

C. neither

15. $y = \cos\dfrac{1}{4}x$
(47)

A. even symmetry

B. odd symmetry

C. neither

Answer the following question.

16. Tell whether the function $y = \sin x + 3\cos x$ is periodic or non-periodic.
(48)

Without using a calculator, solve for f in each equation below. Give exact answers. (All angles are in radians.)

17. $f = \cos\left(-\dfrac{3\pi}{2}\right)$
(44)

18. $f = \arcsin\left(-\dfrac{\sqrt{3}}{2}\right)$
(49)

19. $f = \cos\left(\cos^{-1}\left(\dfrac{\pi}{4}\right)\right)$
(49)

Select the answer for each trig equation below. Make sure your choice includes possible solutions. (All angles are in degrees.)

20. $\sin\theta = -1$
(50)

A. $\theta = -90° + n360°$

B. $\theta = 0° + n180°$

C. $\theta = 90° + n360°$

D. $\theta = 180° + n360°$

E. $\theta = 90° + n360°$
$\theta = -90° + n360°$

21. $2\cos\alpha = \sqrt{3}$
(50)

    A. $\alpha = 60° + n360°$ B. $\alpha = 30° + n360°$ C. $\alpha = 30° + n360°$
            $\alpha = -60° + n360°$ $\alpha = 150° + n360°$ $\alpha = -30° + n360°$

    D. $\alpha = 60° + n360°$ E. $\alpha = 45° + n360°$
            $\alpha = 120° + n360°$ $\alpha = -45° + n360°$

Solve each trig equation below for $0 \le x < 2\pi$. (All angles are in radians.)

22. $\sqrt{2}\sin x = 1$
(50)

23. $4\cos\left(x + \dfrac{\pi}{6}\right) = 2$
(50)

Solve the word problem below.

24. Kari just got a new car with tires that are 21 inches in diameter. If her wheels are spinning at a rate of 800
(44) revolutions per minute, how fast is she going in miles per hour? Round your answer to a whole number.

Chapter 8 Test

Tell whether each sentence below is true or false.

1. The word "identity" means that the expressions on each side of the equals sign are always equal for any
(51) value of x (as long as x is defined for each function).

2. One of the best ways to simplify a tough trig expression is to first change all of the trig ratios to sines and
(53) cosines.

Answer each question below.

3. Select the expression below that is identical to $\tan(-\theta)\tan\left(\dfrac{\pi}{2}-\theta\right)$.
(52)

    A. 1   B. $\tan^2\theta$ C. -1

    D. $\cot^2\theta$ E. 0

4. Select the expression below that is identical to $\dfrac{1}{1-\cos x}+\dfrac{1}{1+\cos x}$.
(52)

    A. $2\sec^2\theta$ B. 1   C. $2\cos^2 x$

    D. $2\sin^2 x$ E. $2\csc^2 x$

5. Select the expression below that is identical to $\dfrac{1}{2}\sec^2\alpha\cot\alpha$.
(56)

    A. $\csc 2\alpha$ B. $\dfrac{1}{2}$ C. $\cos 2\alpha$

    D. $\sin\dfrac{\alpha}{2}$ E. $\cos\dfrac{\alpha}{2}$

Select the simplified form of each given expression below.

6. $\csc x\sin^2\left(\dfrac{\pi}{2}-x\right)\tan x$
(53)

    A. $\tan x$ B. $\cos x$ C. $\tan^2 x$

    D. 1   E. $\sin x$

7. $\dfrac{1+\cos\alpha}{\sin\alpha}+\dfrac{\sin\alpha}{1+\cos\alpha}$
(53)

    A. $\tan\alpha$ B. $2\sec\alpha$ C. $2\sin\alpha$

    D. $2\csc\alpha$ E. $2\cos\alpha$

8. $\dfrac{\sec\theta}{\sin\theta}-\dfrac{\sin\theta}{\cos\theta}$
(53)

    A. $\tan\theta$ B. 1   C. $\sec\theta$

    D. $\csc\theta$ E. $\cot\theta$

Use your knowledge of trig identities (not a calculator) to find each trig value below.

9. If $\cos\theta = \dfrac{1}{3}$, find $\sec\theta$.
(51)

10. If $\csc\alpha = \dfrac{5}{2}$, find $\sec\alpha\cot\alpha$.
(53)

Find the exact value of each trig function below.

11. $\sin(x-y)$ if $\sin x = \dfrac{7}{25}$, $\cos x = \dfrac{24}{25}$, $\sin y = \dfrac{3}{5}$ and $\cos y = \dfrac{4}{5}$.
(54)

12. $\cos(x+y)$ if $\sin x = \dfrac{12}{13}$, $\cos x = \dfrac{5}{13}$, $\sin y = \dfrac{8}{17}$ and $\cos y = \dfrac{15}{17}$.
(54)

Use double-angle identities to find the exact value of each trig function below.

13. $\sin 2\alpha$ if $\sin\alpha = \dfrac{5}{13}$, $\cos\alpha = \dfrac{12}{13}$
(56)

14. $\cos 2\theta$ if $\sin\theta = \dfrac{2}{5}$
(56)

Use half-angle identities to find the exact value of each trig function below.

15. $\sin\dfrac{\alpha}{2}$ if $\cos\alpha = \dfrac{7}{9}$ (assume $\sin\dfrac{\alpha}{2}$ is positive)
(57)

16. $\cos\dfrac{\alpha}{2}$ if $\cos\alpha = -\dfrac{31}{49}$ (assume $\cos\dfrac{\alpha}{2}$ is negative)
(57)

Solve each trig equation below. (All angles are in radians.)

17. $4\cos x - 4\sin^2 x + 5 = 0$ for $0 \le x < \pi$
(58)

18. $2\cos^2 x + \cos x = 1$ for $0 \le x \le \pi$
(58)

19. $2\sin x\cos x - \sqrt{3}\cos x = 0$ for $0 \le x < \pi$
(58)

Select the answer for each question below.

20. The graph of the line with equation $ax + by = 1$ is shown below. Which of the following must be true?
(8)

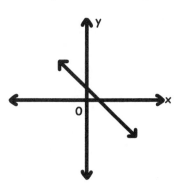

A. $a < 0$ and $b < 0$ B. $a > 0$ and $b > 0$ C. $a > 0$ and $b < 0$

D. $a < 0$ and $b > 0$ E. $a = 0$ and $b > 0$

21. Which of the following is an even function (has even symmetry)?
(47)

A. $f(x) = \log_3 x$ B. $f(x) = \sin x$ C. $f(x) = x^3 + 4$

D. $f(x) = 2^x$ E. $f(x) = \sec x$

22. If $x = \dfrac{\cot \theta}{3}$ and $y = \dfrac{\sin \theta}{\cos \theta}$, what is y in terms of x?
(53)

A. $3x$ B. $\dfrac{1}{3x}$ C. 1

D. $\dfrac{3}{x}$ E. $\dfrac{x}{3}$

23. If $x + y = 90°$ and x and y are positive, then $\dfrac{\sin x}{\cos y} = ?$
(51)

A. 1 B. $\dfrac{1}{2}$ C. 0

D. -1 E. It cannot be determined from the information given

Solve the word problem below. Do not use a calculator.

24. The function $h(t) = 25 - 10\cos\left(\dfrac{\pi}{3}t\right)$ gives the height above the ground, in feet, of a passenger on a Ferris
(46)
wheel t minutes after the ride begins. During one revolution of the Ferris wheel, for how many minutes is the passenger at least 25 feet above the ground?

Chapter 9 Test

Tell whether each sentence below is true or false.

1. A vector is a special number that can be used to represent both magnitude and direction.
(59)

2. Using vectors, forces that push (or pull) an object in different directions can be added together to figure out
(61) the strength and direction of the combined force.

If $p = 12i - 4j$ **and** $q = -7i + 8j$ **, calculate the value of each expression below. Estimate any irrational answers to one decimal place.**

3. $p - 2q$
(60)

4. $\|p + q\|$
(59)

Answer each question below. Estimate any irrational numbers to one decimal place.

5. Find the components of a vector **u** with magnitude 10 and direction angle $\theta = 54°$.
(60)

6. Find the magnitude and direction angle of $v = -7i + 3j$.
(60)

7. Find the unit vector that's in the same direction as $w = 20i - 21j$.
(60)

8. Add the two forces below to find the resultant force.
(61)

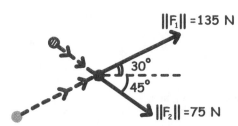

9. A cart full of packages weighing 180 pounds is rolling down a ramp 12 feet long at an incline of $25°$. (The
(61) force applied by gravity is equal to the weight of the cart and the packages.) Find the work done by gravity as the cart moves the length of the ramp. Assume that friction is not a factor.

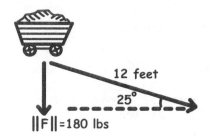

For each pair of parametric equations below, eliminate the parameter and select the direct relationship between x and y.

10. $x = 3 + 2t$, $y = -1 + 4t$
(62)

    A. $y = \dfrac{1}{2}x + \dfrac{7}{2}$ B. $y = 8x + 11$ C. $y = 2x - 7$

    D. $y = 8x + 1$ E. $y = 8x^2 + 10x - 3$

11. $x = 3 - t$, $y = t^2 - 2t$
(62)

    A. $y = -x^2 + 2x + 3$ B. $y = x^2 - 8x + 15$ C. $y = 3 - x$

    D. $y = -x^3 + 5x^2 - 6x$ E. $y = x^2 - 4x + 3$

For each pair of polar coordinates below, select the correct conversion into rectangular coordinates. Don't use the polar conversion function on your calculator.

12. $E(10, 45°)$
(63)

    A. $(5\sqrt{3}, 5\sqrt{3})$ B. $(-5\sqrt{2}, 5\sqrt{2})$ C. $(5\sqrt{2}, -5\sqrt{2})$

    D. $(5\sqrt{2}, 5\sqrt{2})$ E. $(\sqrt{10}, \sqrt{10})$

13. $F(18, 240°)$
(63)

    A. $(-9, -9\sqrt{3})$ B. $(-9, 9\sqrt{3})$ C. $(-9\sqrt{3}, -9)$

    D. $(9\sqrt{3}, 9)$ E. $(9, -9\sqrt{3})$

For each pair of rectangular coordinates below, select the correct conversion into polar coordinates rounded to 1 decimal place. Don't use the polar conversion function on your calculator.

14. $J(14, 8)$
(63)

    A. $(16.1, 29.7°)$ B. $(22, 29.7°)$ C. $(16.1, -29.7°)$

    D. $(-16.1, 330.3°)$ E. $(-16.1, 29.7°)$

15. $K(-25, 3)$
(63)

    A. $(-25.2, -173.2°)$ B. $(-22, 6.84°)$ C. $(25.2, -173.2°)$

    D. $(-25.2, 173.2°)$ E. $(25.2, 173.2°)$

Select the graph for each equation below.

16. $x = 2 - t$, $y = -4 + 3t$
(62)

A. 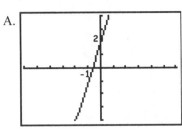   B. 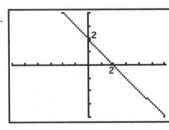   C.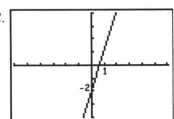

D. 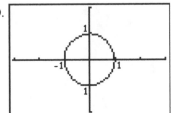   E.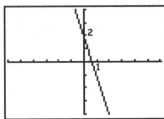

17. $r = \theta$
(63)

A. 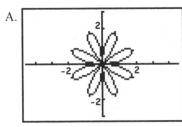   B. 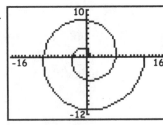   C.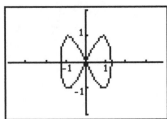

D. 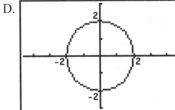   E.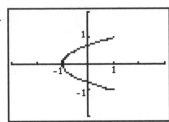

Solve each trig equation below for $0 \le x < \pi$. (All angles are in radians.)

18. $\sqrt{2}\cos x \tan x - \tan x = 0$
(58)

19. $2\sin x - 4\csc x = -2$
(58)

Answer each question below.

20. If the graph of the equation $y = mx + 2$ has points in the 3rd quadrant, then which of the following must be
(8)   true for m?

    A. $m = -2$ B. $m < 0$ C. $m = 0$

    D. $m > 0$ E. $0 < m < 2$

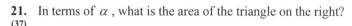
21. In terms of α, what is the area of the triangle on the right?
(37)

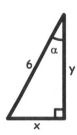

    A. $18\sin^2\alpha$ B. $\dfrac{1}{2}\tan\alpha$

    C. $18\sin\alpha\cos\alpha$ D. $36\sin\alpha\cos\alpha$

    E. $\dfrac{1}{2}\alpha$

22. If $\sqrt{x+12} = \sqrt{x} + 2$, then what is the value of x?
(31)

23. A line has parametric equations $x = 7t - 2$, and $y = -4 + 3t$. What is the slope of the line representing y as
(62) a function of x?

Solve the word problem below.

24. To get to her friend's house, Sandra walked along the sidewalk in her neighborhood. If she walked 100
(60) yards at a direction 45° north of east and then turned to walk 400 yards straight east, how many yards and
in what direction would she need to walk if she wanted to walk straight home without having to make any
turns? Round any irrational answers to one decimal place.

Chapter 10 Test

Tell whether each sentence below is true or false.

1. Systems of equations can be solved by the substitution or the elimination method.
(64)

2. A matrix can have a different number of rows than it has columns.
(68)

Answer each question below. Estimate any irrational answers to one decimal place.

3. Find the magnitude and direction angle of $\mathbf{p} = 42\mathbf{i} + 35\mathbf{j}$.
(60)

4. Find the unit vector that's in the same direction as $\mathbf{q} = 35\mathbf{i} - 12\mathbf{j}$.
(60)

Solve each system of equations below.

5.
(64)
$\begin{cases} x - 4y = -26 \\ 3x + 2y = 6 \end{cases}$

6.
(65)
$\begin{cases} y = x^2 + 3x - 5 \\ 2x - y = -7 \end{cases}$

7.
(65)
$\begin{cases} -5x + 4y - 3z = -21 \\ -2y + z = 7 \\ -4z = 12 \end{cases}$

Find the value of each determinant below.

8.
(66)
$\begin{vmatrix} 4 & 3 \\ -12 & -8 \end{vmatrix}$

9.
(67)
$\begin{vmatrix} -11 & 5 & 8 \\ 2 & -3 & 4 \\ -6 & 7 & 0 \end{vmatrix}$

Solve each system of equations below using determinants.

10.
(66)
$\begin{cases} -2x + 7y = 46 \\ 9x - 6y = -3 \end{cases}$

11.
(67)
$\begin{cases} 3x - 10y = -9 \\ -9x + 5y = 7 \end{cases}$

12.
(68)
$\begin{cases} 6x + 8y - z = -23 \\ -12x - y + 3z = 68 \\ -4x + 3y - 5z = -16 \end{cases}$

If $A = \begin{bmatrix} 14 & -7 & 10 \\ 9 & 2 & -17 \\ -6 & 3 & -4 \end{bmatrix}$, $B = \begin{bmatrix} -5 & 9 & -2 \\ 4 & -11 & 18 \\ 3 & -6 & 7 \end{bmatrix}$ and $C = \begin{bmatrix} 12 & -4 & 16 \\ 1 & 5 & -3 \end{bmatrix}$, **calculate the value of each expression**

below.

13. $A + B$
(69)

14. $-4B$
(69)

15. CA
(69)

Select the graph for each system of inequalities below.

16.
(70)
$$\begin{cases} 4x + 3y \leq -12 \\ 2x - y \geq -2 \end{cases}$$

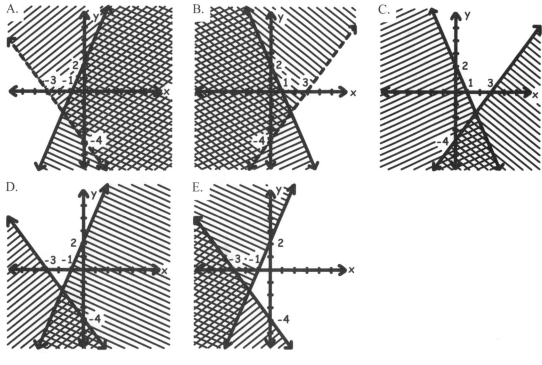

17.
(70)
$$\begin{cases} y > -x^2 \\ x + 2y \geq -4 \end{cases}$$

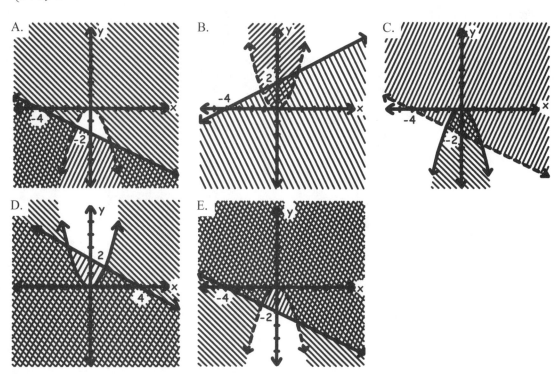

Use your knowledge of trig identities (not a calculator) to find each trig value below.

18. If $\tan(-\alpha) = -5$, find $\cot\alpha$
(51)

19. If $\csc\theta = \dfrac{4}{3}$, find $\sin\theta + \sin\theta\cot^2\theta$
(58)

Select the answer for each question below.

20. The graph of which of the following functions is symmetric with respect to the origin?
(4)

    A. $f(x) = e^{-x}$ B. $g(x) = (x+6)^3$ C. $h(x) = (x-3)^2$

    D. $P(x) = 2x^3 - 4$ E. $Q(x) = \dfrac{1}{2}\sin x$

21. If $\cos(110 - 4x) = \sin(3x)$, then $x = ?$
(52)

    A. $0°$ B. $10°$ C. $15°$

    D. $20°$ E. $25°$

Answer each question below.

22. If $g(x) = x + 3$ and $h(x) = 9 - x^2$. What is the maximum value of $h(g(x))$?
(10)

23. If $x = \arctan\left(-\dfrac{3}{4}\right)$ and $x + y = 210°$, then $\cos y = ?$ Estimate your answer to two decimal places.
(49)

Solve the word problem below.

24. For his troops' popcorn fundraiser sale, Mike sold caramel corn for $10, buttered microwave popcorn for
(65) $8, and lightly buttered microwave popcorn for $7. By the end of the fundraiser, he had sold 400 items and made $3,272. If he sold twice as many lightly buttered microwave popcorn boxes as the buttered popcorn, how many of each type of popcorn did he sell?

Chapter 11 Test

Tell whether each sentence below is true or false.

1. In geometry, a parabola is defined as the collection (locus) of points that are the same distance from a point
(72) (called the focus) and a line (called the directrix).

2. In geometry, an ellipse is defined as the collection (locus) of points whose distances from two fixed points
(73) (the foci) always have a constant sum.

Solve each system of equations below.

3.
(64)
$\begin{cases} 6x + 2y = 1 \\ -3x + 4y = -3 \end{cases}$

4.
(65)
$\begin{cases} y = x^2 - 2x - 3 \\ 6x + y = 2 \end{cases}$

Select the equation for each circle below.

5. Center at $(4, 2)$ with radius 9
(71)

    A. $(x-4)^2 + (y-2)^2 = 9$ B. $(x+4)^2 + (y+2)^2 = 9^2$ C. $(x-4)^2 + (y-2)^2 = 81$

    D. $(x-2)^2 + (y-4)^2 = 81$ E. $(x+4)^2 + (y+2)^2 = 9$

6. Center at $(3, -6)$ and tangent to the x-axis.
(71)

    A. $(x-3)^2 + (y+6)^2 = 36$ B. $(x-3)^2 + (y+6)^2 = 3^2$ C. $(x+3)^2 + (y-6)^2 = 9$

    D. $(x+3)^2 + (y-6)^2 = 36$ E. $(x+6)^2 + (y-3)^2 = 36$

Answer each question below.

7. Select the focus and directrix for the parabola: $y = \dfrac{1}{8}(x+1)^2$.
(72)

    A.   Focus $(1, 2)$; Directrix $x = -2$ B.   Focus $(2, -1)$; Directrix $y = 1$

    C.   Focus $(-1, 2)$; Directrix $x = -3$ D.   Focus $(-1, 2)$; Directrix $y = -2$

    E.   Focus $\left(-1, \dfrac{1}{2}\right)$; Directrix $y = -\dfrac{1}{2}$

8. Select the focus and directrix for the parabola: $x = -3y^2 - 24y - 46$.
(72)

    A.   Focus $\left(2, \dfrac{47}{12}\right)$; Directrix $x = \dfrac{49}{12}$ B.   Focus $(-1, -4)$; Directrix $x = 5$

    C.   Focus $\left(2, -\dfrac{49}{12}\right)$; Directrix $y = -\dfrac{47}{12}$ D.   Focus $\left(\dfrac{23}{12}, 4\right)$; Directrix $y = \dfrac{25}{12}$

    E.   Focus $\left(\dfrac{23}{12}, -4\right)$; Directrix $x = \dfrac{25}{12}$

9. Select the equation for the ellipse whose center is at $(-3,1)$, the length of the major axis is 10 units, and the
(73) length of the minor axis is 6 units.

A. $\dfrac{(x+3)^2}{20^2}+\dfrac{(y-1)^2}{12^2}=1$ B. $\dfrac{(x+3)^2}{5^2}+\dfrac{(y-1)^2}{3^2}=1$ C. $\dfrac{(x-3)^2}{25}+\dfrac{(y+1)^2}{9}=1$

D. $\dfrac{(x-3)^2}{10^2}+\dfrac{(y+1)^2}{6^2}=1$ E. $\dfrac{x^2}{400}+\dfrac{y^2}{144}=1$

Answer the questions for each hyperbola below.

10. Select the center and vertices of $\dfrac{y^2}{81}-\dfrac{x^2}{16}=1$.
(74)

A. Center $(0,0)$; Vertices $(0,-4)$, $(0,4)$ B. Center $(9,0)$; Vertices $(-4,0)$, $(4,0)$

C. Center $(0,4)$; Vertices $(0,9)$, $(9,0)$ D. Center $(0,0)$; Vertices $(-9,0)$, $(9,0)$

E. Center $(0,0)$; Vertices $(0,-9)$, $(0,9)$

11. Select the center and vertices of $\dfrac{(x+3)^2}{36}-\dfrac{(y-5)^2}{9}=1$.
(74)

A. Center $(-3,5)$; Vertices $(5,-9)$, $(5,3)$ B. Center $(3,-5)$; Vertices $(-6,0)$, $(6,0)$

C. Center $(-3,5)$; Vertices $(-3,-1)$, $(-3,11)$ D. Center $(-3,5)$; Vertices $(-9,5)$, $(3,5)$

E. Center $(0,0)$; Vertices $(6,0)$, $(0,3)$

Select the standard form for each conic section equation below.

12. $x^2+6x-3y+18=0$
(75)

A. $y=3(x+1)^2-3$ B. $y-\dfrac{1}{3}=3(x-1)^2$ C. $y-3=3(x+3)^2$

D. $y-3=\dfrac{1}{3}(x+3)^2$ E. $y-3=-3(x+3)^2$

13. $16x^2-9y^2-64x-18y=89$
(75)

A. $9(x-2)^2-16(y+1)^2=144$ B. $\dfrac{(x-2)^2}{3^2}-\dfrac{(y+1)^2}{4^2}=1$ C. $\dfrac{(x-2)^2}{4^2}-\dfrac{(y+1)^2}{3^2}=1$

D. $\dfrac{x^2}{9}+\dfrac{y^2}{16}=1$ E. $y-16=4(x-2)^2$

Select whether each conic section below is a circle, parabola, ellipse or hyperbola without completing the square.

14. $25x^2 + 25y^2 - 200x - 50y + 31 = 0$
(75)

    A. Circle   B. Parabola   C. Ellipse   D. Hyperbola

15. $5x - 7y^2 + 98y - 62 = 0$
(75)

    A. Circle   B. Parabola   C. Ellipse   D. Hyperbola

Select the correct translation or rotation for each conic section equation below.

16. If the x-axis is translated 5 places up and the y-axis 12 places to the left, the equation
(76)
$\dfrac{(x+12)^2}{49} - \dfrac{(y-5)^2}{25} = 1$ changes to which of the following?

    A. $\dfrac{(x'-12)^2}{7^2} + \dfrac{(y'+5)^2}{5^2} = 1$ B. $\dfrac{(x'+5)^2}{49} - \dfrac{(y'+12)^2}{25} = 1$ C. $\dfrac{x'^2}{49} - \dfrac{y'^2}{25} = 1$

    D. $\dfrac{12x'^2}{49} - \dfrac{5y'^2}{16} = 1$ E. $\dfrac{x'^2}{5^2} - \dfrac{y'^2}{7^2} = 1$

17. If the axes are rotated $45°$, the equation $xy = 18$ changes to which of the following?
(76)

    A. $\dfrac{(x')^2}{6} - \dfrac{(y')^2}{6} = 1$ B. $\dfrac{(x')^2}{36} + \dfrac{(y')^2}{36} = 1$ C. $x'y' = 36$

    D. $\dfrac{(x')^2}{6^2} - \dfrac{(y')^2}{6^2} = 1$ E. $y' = \dfrac{18}{x'}$

Select the answer for each question below.

18. Which of the following is not a factor of $x^5 + 2x^4 + 3x^3 + 6x^2 - 4x - 8$?
(13)

    A. $x^2 + 4$ B. $x + 1$ C. $x - 2i$

    D. $x - 1$ E. $x - 2$

19. If $\csc\theta > 0$ and $\cot\theta < 0$ then in which quadrant does θ lie?
(47)

    A. I   B. II   C. III

    D. II or III   E. IV

Answer each question below.

20. If $16x^2 - 24x + k = 0$ has two roots (a double root) equal to $\dfrac{3}{4}$, $k = ?$
(15)

21. If $8.2^p = 10.5^q$, then $\dfrac{p}{q} = ?$ Estimate your answer to two decimal places.
(26)

22. If $8^x = 12$, then $24^x = ?$ Estimate your answer to one decimal place.
(30)

23. What is the length of the major axis of the ellipse $\dfrac{9(x+5)^2}{4^2} + \dfrac{(y-9)^2}{2^2} = 1$?
(73)

Solve the word problem below.

24. A ferry boat departed from port and traveled at a rate of 10 miles per hour at an angle $30°$ north of east
(61) across a large river. If the current is flowing at a rate of 4 miles per hour straight south, what is the speed
and direction of the boat in the water? Round any irrational answers to one decimal place.

Chapter 12 Test

Tell whether each sentence below is true or false.

1. To calculate probability, take the number of favorable outcomes divided by the total number of outcomes.
(80)

2. The mean is the number that's exactly in the middle of a group of data.
(83)

Answer each question below.

3. Find the 8th term in an arithmetic sequence with $a_1 = 3$ and a common difference (d) of 6 .
(77)

4. Find the common ratio (r) in the geometric sequence: $1, -\dfrac{3}{4}, \dfrac{9}{16}, \dfrac{-27}{64}...$
(77)

5. If the common ratio (r) of a geometric sequence is 2 and $g_{11} = 6,144$, find the first term of the sequence.
(77)

6. The first 70 terms of an arithmetic sequence are $9 + 13 + 17 + ... + 285$. Find the sum.
(78)

Find the sum of each infinite geometric series, or indicate that the sum does not exist.

7. $3 + 9 + 27 + 81 + ...$
(79)

8. $15 + 6 + \dfrac{12}{5} + \dfrac{24}{25} + ...$
(79)

Calculate the number of permutations in each problem below.

9. How many possible ways can a group of 8 people line up in front of a grocery's check-out booth?
(81)

10. How many unique words can be made by arranging the letters of the word NANNY? (The words do not
(81) have to be real words in any dictionary but each word must use every letter.)

Calculate the number of combinations in each problem below.

11. How many different 9-member boards of directors can be formed from a group of 14 candidates?
(81)

12. Josh has 10 favorite CDs in his classical music collection. If he wishes to take 6 CDs on a field trip, how
(81) many different combinations of 6 CDs are possible?

Answer each question below. Write your answer as a fraction.

13. A kitchen drawer has 7 spoons, 5 forks, and 3 knives. Without looking, Miranda selects one piece of
(82) silverware from the drawer. What is the probability that the chosen piece is a fork?

14. A bowl contains 6 apples, 2 oranges and 4 bananas. Without looking, James chose one piece of fruit for
(82) himself. What is the probability that he chose an apple or a banana?

15. A hotel gives every customer who makes a reservation a confirmation code. How many different
(80) confirmation codes can be created if each code has 4 letters followed by 2 numbers?

16. The probability that Jeff will be accepted to Green Valley College is $\dfrac{3}{4}$, and, the probability that Justin will
(82) be accepted to Blue Ridge College is $\dfrac{2}{5}$. What is the probability that Justin will be accepted and Jeff will not?

17. There are 4 romantic novels and 6 adventurous novels on a book shelf. Without looking, Carmen chooses 2
(82) novels out of the shelf. What is the probability that she chooses 2 romantic novels?

Use the following information to answer each question below. Estimate any irrational answers to one decimal place.

The SAT math scores obtained by a population of 13 students were recorded as follows: 580, 420, 710, 365, 640, 570, 750, 485, 610, 515, 640, 725, 590.

18. Find the mean and range of the SAT math scores.
(84)

19. Find the median and mode of the SAT math scores.
(83)

20. Find the standard deviation of the SAT math scores.
(84)

Select the answer for the following question.

21. If $m(x) = \sqrt[3]{x}$ and $m(n(x)) = -2\sqrt[3]{x}$, then $n(x) = ?$
(31)

    A. $-x^6$ B. $2x^3$ C. $\dfrac{x}{2}$

    D. $2x^{-3}$ E. $-8x$

Answer the following question.

22. In an arithmetic sequence, $a_6 = 31$ and $a_{11} = 56$. What is a_{200}?
(77)

23. Ann's average score on the first 3 tests of her Trigonometry course was 76. If she makes a 92 on the 4th
(83) test, what will her new test average be?

Solve the word problem below.

24. The cost of an annual gym membership can be represented by the function $C(t) = 300 - 5t$ where t is the
(78) number of years that one has belonged to the gym. If Jeffrey has been a member for 5 years, what is the total amount of money that he has paid to the gym over the past 5 years (after he has paid his annual fee for the sixth year)?

Chapter 13 Test

Tell whether each sentence below is true or false.

1. The process of finding the derivative for a function is called differentiation.
(85)

2. The equation for a definite integral is $\int_a^b f'(x)dx = f(b) - f(a)$.
(88)

Calculate the number of permutations or combinations in each problem below.

3. A restaurant offers a lunch special where you can choose any 3 of a total of 9 dishes. How many different combinations are possible?
(81)

4. In a running competition, 14 participants are competing for the first, second and third prize. How many possibilities are there for selecting the winners for the three prizes?
(81)

Select the derivative of each function below.

5. $f(x) = 5x - 2$
(85)

    A. $f'(x) = -2$ B. $\dfrac{df}{dx} = \dfrac{5}{2}x^2 - 2$ C. $f'(x) = 5$

    D. $\dfrac{df}{dx} = 5x^2 - 2$ E. $f' = \dfrac{1}{5}x - 2$

6. $g(x) = 12x^2$
(85)

    A. $\dfrac{dg}{dx} = 24x$ B. $g'(x) = 4x^3$ C. $\dfrac{dg}{dx} = 24x^3$

    D. $g'(x) = 12$ E. $g' = 12x$

Use the following information to answer each question below.

In a random sample, 16 residents of Clarendon Park were asked how many hours they spent using the Internet in the previous week. Their answers were as follows: 13, 15, 28, 30, 26, 12, 9, 11, 7, 24, 15, 8, 16, 13, 17, 23.

7. Find the mean and the range for the sample. Estimate your answers to 1 decimal place.
(84)

8. Find the standard deviation and the median for the sample. Estimate any irrational answers to two decimal places.
(84)

Find the slope of the tangent line at the labeled point in each graph below.

9.
(86)

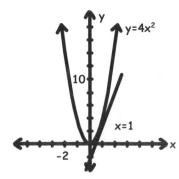

10.
(86)

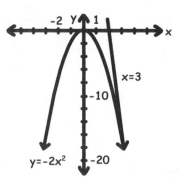

Answer each question below.

11. Given $h(x) = x^3 - 75x$ and $\dfrac{dh}{dx} = 3x^2 - 75$, select the local maximum and minimum of $h(x)$.
(86)

    A. Local Max: $(-5, 0)$; Local Min: $(5, 0)$ B. Local Max: $(-5, -250)$; Local Min: $(5, 250)$

    C. Local Max: $(5, 250)$; Local Min: $(-5, 250)$ D. Local Max: $(5\sqrt{3}, 150)$; Local Min: $(0, 0)$

    E. Local Max: $(-5, 250)$; Local Min $(5, -250)$

12. Given $u(x) = -2x^3 + 9x^2 + 24x + 3$ and $u'(x) = -6x^2 + 18x + 24$, select the local maximum and minimum
(86) of $u(x)$.

    A. Local Max: $(1, 34)$; Local Min: $(4, 115)$ B. Local Max: $(4, -10)$; Local Min: $(-1, 115)$

    C. Local Max: $(-1, -10)$; Local Min: $(-4, 179)$ D. Local Max: $(4, 115)$; Local Min: $(-1, -10)$

    E. Local Max: $(1, -10)$; Local Min: $(4, -115)$

Select the answer for each question below.

13. A baseball is thrown downward from the top of a building with an initial velocity of 7 feet/sec.
(87) (Remember, the acceleration of a falling object is 32 ft/sec^2.) Select the function that describes the
relationship between the velocity (v) of the baseball and time (t).

    A. $v = 32t + 7$ B. $v = 32t$ C. $v = 16t^2 + 7$

    D. $v = 32$ E. $v = 16t^2 + 7t$

14. A can is thrown downward with an initial velocity of 12 feet/sec from the top of a cliff. (Remember, the
(87) acceleration of a falling object is 32 ft/sec^2.) Select the function that describes the relationship between the
distance the can travels (d) and time (t).

    A. $d = 16t^2 + 12$ B. $d = 32t + 12$ C. $d = 16t^2 + 12t$

    D. $d = 32$ E. $d = 32t$

Answer each question below.

15. Find the area shown below. (Hint: The indefinite integral of $y = x^2$ is $y = \dfrac{x^3}{3} + C$.)
(88)

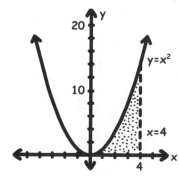

16. Find the area shown below. (Hint: The indefinite integral of $y = 3x^{\frac{1}{2}}$ is $y = 2x^{\frac{3}{2}} + C$.)
(88)

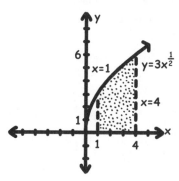

Calculate each of the following limits.

17. $\displaystyle\lim_{x \to 2}(x^2 + 6x - 5)$
(85)

18. $\displaystyle\lim_{x \to -4}\dfrac{x^2 - 16}{x + 4}$
(85)

Select the answer for each question below.

19. The solution set of $8x - 6y < -1$ lies in which quadrants?
(70)

    A. I only   B. I and II   C. II, III and IV
    D. I, III, and IV   E. I, II, and III

20. What is the range of $f(x) = -5\sin(4x - \pi) + 2$?
(45)

    A. $0 \le y \le 2\pi$ B. $-3 \le y \le 7$ C. $-\dfrac{3}{4} \le y \le \dfrac{7}{4}$

    D. All real numbers   E. $-5 \le y \le 5$

Answer each question below.

21. If $\sqrt[3]{n} = 5.18$, then $\sqrt[3]{7n} = ?$ Estimate your answer to 1 decimal place.
(31)

22. If 6, $\dfrac{29}{2}$, and 23 are the first three terms of an arithmetic sequence, what is the sum of the first 18 terms of
(78) the sequence?

23. The boys' basketball team scored an average of 69 points per game in their first 5 games of the season. The
(83) girls' basketball team scored an average of 54 points per game in their first 3 games. What was the average of points scored in all 8 games? Estimate your answer to 2 decimal places.

Solve the word problem below.

24. The position of a bucket falling down a well can be represented by the function $h(t) = 16t^2$ where t is time
(85) in seconds and $h(t)$ is measured in feet. Based on this function, what is the velocity of the bucket after it has fallen for 4 seconds?

Chapter 14 Test

Tell whether each sentence below is true or false.

1. With the Binomial Theorem, we can find a specific term (such as the 3rd term) of an expansion of $(x+y)^n$.
(90)

2. An ambiguous case occurs when you're trying to solve a triangle and there are two possible answers.
(92)

Answer each question below.

3. What is the probability of getting an even number when rolling a die?
(82)

4. Assuming there is a 0.5 probability that any newborn baby will be a girl, what is the probability that a
(82) woman will have a girl, then a boy, and then another girl?

Using the Binomial Theorem, select the correct expansion for each binomial below.

5. $(x+y)^{10}$
(90)

A. $x^{10}+10x^9y+36x^8y^2+84x^7y^3+126x^6y^4+210x^5y^5+126x^4y^6+84x^3y^7+36x^2y^8+10xy^9+y^{10}$

B. $x+10xy+45x^2y^2+120x^3y^3+210x^4y^4+252x^5y^5+210x^6y^6+120x^7y^7+45x^8y^8+10x^9y^9+y^{10}$

C. $x^{10}+3x^8y^4+3x^4y^8+y^{10}$

D. $x^{10}+2x^5y^5+y^{10}$

E. $x^{10}+10x^9y+45x^8y^2+120x^7y^3+210x^6y^4+252x^5y^5+210x^4y^6+120x^3y^7+45x^2y^8+10xy^9+y^{10}$

6. $(a-b)^9$
(90)

A. $a^9-2a^5b^5+b^9$

B. $a^9-9a^8b+36a^7b^2-56a^6b^3+70a^5b^4-84a^4b^5+56a^3b^6-36a^2b^7+9ab^8-b^9$

C. $a^9-3a^6b^3+3a^3b^6-b^9$

D. $a^9-9a^8b+36a^7b^2-84a^6b^3+126a^5b^4-126a^4b^5+84a^3b^6-36a^2b^7+9ab^8-b^9$

E. $a^3+9a^2b^9+36a^3b^8+84a^4b^7+126a^5b^6+126a^6b^5+84a^7b^4+36a^8b^3+9a^9b^2+b^3$

Select the indicated term for each binomial expansion below.

7. The 4th term of $(x+y)^{18}$
(90)

A. $3,060x^{14}y^4$ B. $816x^3y^{15}$ C. $816x^{15}y^3$

D. $742x^6y^{12}$ E. $8,568x^{15}y^3$

8.
(90) The middle term of $\left(4x - \dfrac{1}{4}y\right)^6$?

A. $-20x^3y^3$ B. $20x^3y^3$ C. $0.31x^3y^3$

D. $1,280x^3y^3$ E. $-14x^4y^4$

Calculate each of the following limits.

9.
(85) $\lim\limits_{x\to 2}(-x^3 - 7x^2 + 9)$

10.
(85) $\lim\limits_{x\to -3}\dfrac{x^2 + 3x}{x^2 - 4x - 21}$

Using synthetic division, select the quotient for each polynomial division below.

11.
(91) $\dfrac{2x^3 - 3x^2 - 9x + 10}{x + 2}$

A. Quotient: $2x^2 - 5x$; Remainder: 6

B. Quotient: $2x^2 - 7x + 5$; No remainder

C. Quotient: $2x^2 + 5x - 7$; No remainder

D. Quotient: $2x^2 + x - 7$; Remainder: -4

E. Quotient: $-2x^2 + 7x + 5$; No remainder

12.
(91) $\dfrac{x^3 - 34x + 42}{x - 5}$

A. Quotient: $x^2 - 5x - 9$; Remainder: 87

B. Quotient: $-x^2 + 9x - 8$; No remainder

C. Quotient: $x^2 - 6x$; No remainder

D. Quotient: $x^2 - 5x + 9$; Remainder: -3

E. Quotient: $x^2 + 5x - 9$; Remainder: -3

Select the polar (trigonometric) form of each of the following complex numbers. Estimate all quantities to one decimal place.

13. $z = 5 + 12i$
(93)

A. $z = 13(\sin 67.4° + i\cos 67.4°)$

B. $z = 13(\cos 112.6° + i\sin 112.6°)$

C. $z = 13(\cos 67.4° + i\sin 67.4°)$

D. $z = 13(\cos 67.4° - i\sin 67.4°)$

E. $z = 17(\cos 67.4° + i\sin 67.4°)$

14. $z = -24 + (-7i)$
(93)

A. $z = 25(\cos 16.3° + i\sin 16.3°)$

B. $z = 25(\cos 196.3° + i\sin 196.3°)$

C. $z = 25(\cos 196.3° - i\sin 196.3°)$

D. $z = 25(\sin 196.3° + i\cos 196.3°)$

E. $z = 31(\cos 247.4° + i\sin 247.4°)$

Select the answer for each question below.

15.
(93)
$24(\cos 65° + i\sin 65°) \cdot 8(\cos 15° + i\sin 15°)$

    A. $3(\cos 4.3° + i\sin 4.3°)$ B. $32(\cos 80° + i\sin 80°)$ C. $192(\cos 80° + i\sin 80°)$

    D. $192(\cos 975° + i\sin 975°)$ E. $192(\sin 80° + i\cos 80°)$

16.
(93)
$\dfrac{272(\cos 72° + i\sin 72°)}{8(\cos 36° + i\sin 36°)}$

    A. $34(\cos 36° + i\sin 36°)$ B. $34(\sin 36° - i\cos 36°)$ C. $34(\cos 2° + i\sin 2°)$

    D. $2{,}176(\cos 115° + i\sin 115°)$ E. $264(\cos 2° + i\sin 2°)$

17.
(94)
$[7(\cos 43° + i\sin 43°)]^3$

    A. $343(\cos 79{,}507° + i\sin 79{,}507°)$ B. $2.3(\cos 14.3° + i\sin 14.3°)$

    C. $343(\cos 129° + i\sin 129°)$ D. $343(\sin 129° - i\cos 129°)$

    E. $21(\cos 129° + i\sin 129°)$

Select the third roots of the complex number below.

18.
(94)
$[512(\cos 72° + i\sin 72°)]$

    A. $170.7(\cos 24° + i\sin 24°)$, $170.7(\cos 144° + i\sin 144°)$, $170.7(\cos 264° + i\sin 264°)$

    B. $8(\cos 24° + i\sin 24°)$, $8(\cos 144° + i\sin 144°)$, $8(\cos 264° + i\sin 264°)$

    C. $170.7(\cos 4.2° + i\sin 4.2°)$, $170.7(\cos 124.2° + i\sin 124.2°)$, $170.7(\cos 244.2° + i\sin 244.2°)$

    D. $512^3(\cos 75° + i\sin 75°)$

    E. $8(\cos 4.2° + i\sin 4.2°)$, $8(\cos 124.2° + i\sin 124.2°)$, $8(\cos 244.2° + i\sin 244.2°)$

Select the answer for the question below.

A market research study on automobiles contains the following data for sales of automobiles at various prices over the past month.

Price (thousands of dollars) (P)	10	14	18	22	24	28	32
Sales of automobiles (S)	76	48	59	43	36	29	25

19.
(95)
Select the correct regression line and correlation coefficient for the data above. Estimate all quantities to two decimal places.

    A. $S = 90.22P - 2.13$; $r = 0.78$ B. $S = -90.22P + 2.13$; $r = 0.85$

    C. $S = -40.86P + 167.14$; $r = -0.68$ D. $S = -2.13P + 90.22$; $r = -0.92$

    E. $P = -608.68S + 0.89$; $r = -0.93$

Select the answer for each question below.

20. If a function f is an even function and (x, y) is a point on its graph, then which of the following will also be
(4) a point on the graph?

A. $(-x, -y)$ B. $(-x, y)$ C. $(x, -y)$

D. $(-y, -x)$ E. (y, x)

21. A group of 30 juniors and 15 seniors are working in a fund raising drive. The average amount of money
(83) that the group has raised per person is \$20. If the average amount that the seniors have raised is x, give an
expression for the average amount that the juniors have raised in terms of x.

A. $30 - \dfrac{1}{2}x$ B. $125 - 3x$ C. $150 - \dfrac{2}{3}x$

D. $90 - 2x$ E. $900 - 30x$

Answer each question below.

22. An operation is defined on any three real numbers by $r \oplus s \oplus t = r^{s-2t}$. If $3 \oplus 5 \oplus m = 81$, then $m = ?$
(25)

23. If $h(x) = ax^2 + bx + c$, $h(-1) = 13$, and $h(1) = 5$, what is the value of b?
(64)

Solve the word problem below.

24. The points U and V lie on the surface of a cube with sides 8 inches long. What is the maximum distance
(59) that points U and V could be from each other? Round your answer to two decimal places.

find the answers graphically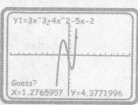

factory costs are a linear function

form... 2, 3, ...

$4n-1$ ... 27, ...

$\left|\begin{matrix} ab \\ cd \end{matrix}\right| =$

CHAPTER TEST ANSWERS

just cross multiply and then subtract

$$\cos 2u = \begin{cases} \cos^2 u - \sin^2 u \\ 2\cos^2 u - 1 \\ 1 - 2\sin^2 u \end{cases}$$

exponential functions

$y = 2^x$

$(-1,2)$ $(1,2)$

$(0,1)$

$y = \left(\frac{1}{2}\right)^x$ or 2^{-x}

reflects across

$x^3 + 2x^2 - 5x - 6 = 0$

$(x-2)(x+3)(x+1) = 0$

Chapter 1 Test
1. True
2. False
3. True
4. Yes
5. No
6. A
7. E
8. C
9. C
10. D
11. A
12. B
13. D
14. B
15. $f(x(2)) = 3$
16. $f(x(7)) = 10$
17. E
18. A
19. B
20. D
21. C
22. A
23. E
24. C

Chapter 2 Test
1. True
2. False
3. B
4. E
5. C
6. D
7. A
8. E
9. 2 turning points
10. 3 turning points
11. E
12. D
13. Remainder $= 1$
14. Remainder $= -3$
15. C
16. B
17. Zero: $x = 2$;
    Local maximum: (0.22, 4.44)
18. Zero: $x = -1.5$;
    Local minimum: (1.54, -1.51)
19. E
20. A
21. Zeros: -4, -4, -4, 0, 6, 6, 6, 6
22. Zeros: $-\dfrac{2}{3}$, $\dfrac{1}{2}$, 1

23. D
24. 30 feet

Chapter 3 Test
1. True
2. True
3. B
4. A
5. Vertical asymptote: $x = -\dfrac{2}{3}$
6. Vertical asymptotes: $x = -2$ and $x = 3$
7. Horizontal asymptote: $y = 0$
8. Horizontal asymptote: $y = -3$
9. E
10. C
11. D
12. B
13. E
14. A
15. B
16. C
17. E
18. B
19. D
20. Zeros: -4, $-\dfrac{3}{2}$, $-\dfrac{3}{2}$, $-\dfrac{3}{2}$, $-\dfrac{3}{2}$, 1, 1
21. Zeros: -2, $-\sqrt{7}$, $\sqrt{7}$
22. $x = -2, 3$
23. $x = -1, 0.5, 4$
24. $21.75

Chapter 4 Test
1. True
2. False
3. 6
4. 9
5. 2.08
6. 1,212.06
7. $x = -\dfrac{2}{3}$
8. $x = 10$
9. 0.8271
10. 1.9534
11. D
12. E
13. $x = -5.01, 5.01$
14. C
15. B
16. E
17. $x = 16$

18. $x = 4$ ($x = -2$ is extraneous)
19. D
20. C
21. B
22. C
23. E
24. 0.0840 milligrams

Chapter 5 Test
1. True
2. True
3. C
4. A
5. D
6. B
7. $y = -10$
8. $y = 9$
9. A
10. C
11. $x = 10$
12. $x = 1$, $x = -2$
13. $t = 9$
14. $x = 6,561$
15. $x = 2, 8$
16. $x = -4, 0$
17. B
18. D
19. D
20. B
21. D
22. A
23. $38
24. 2 seconds

Chapter 6 Test
1. True
2. True
3. 32.9°
4. $\theta = 45°$
5. $\alpha = 60°$
6. $\theta = 60°$
7. $\alpha = 66.4°$
8. $\theta = 56.3°$
9. $HI = 26.5$, $IK = 30.9$, $\angle I = 31°$
10. $ST = 20.5$, $\angle S = 24.4°$, $\angle T = 65.6°$
11. 26.083 inches
12. 193 meters
13. $a = 5.3$
14. $a = 16.2$
15. $\theta = 75.8°$

16. $\alpha = 48.8°$
17. $b = 9.0$
18. $a = 30.3$
19. $\theta = 31.5°$
20. $\alpha = 19.4°$
21. D
22. A
23. C
24. 7.28 feet

Chapter 7 Test
1. True
2. True
3. E
4. C
5. 0.38
6. −0.62
7. C
8. D
9. D
10. E
11. B
12. C
13. E
14. B
15. A
16. Periodic
17. 0
18. $-\dfrac{\pi}{3}$
19. $\dfrac{\pi}{4}$
20. A.
21. C.
22. $x = \dfrac{\pi}{4}, \dfrac{3\pi}{4}$
23. $x = \dfrac{\pi}{6}, \dfrac{3\pi}{2}$
24. 50 miles per hour

Chapter 8 Test
1. True
2. True
3. C
4. E
5. A
6. B
7. D
8. E
9. $\sec \theta = 3$

10. $\sec\alpha\cot\alpha = \dfrac{5}{2}$

11. $\sin(x-y) = -\dfrac{44}{125}$

12. $\cos(x+y) = -\dfrac{21}{221}$

13. $\sin 2\alpha = \dfrac{120}{169}$

14. $\cos 2\theta = \dfrac{17}{25}$

15. $\sin\dfrac{\alpha}{2} = \dfrac{1}{3}$

16. $\cos\dfrac{\alpha}{2} = -\dfrac{3}{7}$

17. $x = \dfrac{2\pi}{3}$

18. $x = \dfrac{\pi}{3},\ \pi$

19. $x = \dfrac{\pi}{3},\ \dfrac{\pi}{2},\ \dfrac{2\pi}{3}$

20. B

21. E

22. B

23. A

24. 3 minutes

Chapter 9 Test

1. True
2. True
3. $\mathbf{p} - 2\mathbf{q} = 26\mathbf{i} - 20\mathbf{j}$
4. $\|\mathbf{p}+\mathbf{q}\| = 6.4$
5. $u_x = 5.9$, $u_y = 8.1$
6. $\|\mathbf{v}\| = 7.6$, $\theta = 156.8°$
7. $\dfrac{20}{29}\mathbf{i} - \dfrac{21}{29}\mathbf{j}$
8. $169.9\mathbf{i} + 14.5\mathbf{j}$
9. 912.9 foot-pounds
10. C
11. E
12. D
13. A
14. A
15. E
16. E
17. B
18. $x = 0,\ \dfrac{\pi}{4}$

19. $x = \dfrac{\pi}{2}$
20. D
21. C
22. $x = 4$
23. $\dfrac{3}{7}$
24. 476.0 yards; 8.5° south of west

Chapter 10 Test

1. True
2. True
3. $\|\mathbf{p}\| = 54.7$, $\theta = 39.8°$
4. $\dfrac{35}{37}\mathbf{i} - \dfrac{12}{37}\mathbf{j}$
5. $x = -2,\ y = 6$
6. $(-4,-1),\ (3,13)$
7. $x = 2,\ y = -5,\ z = -3$
8. 4
9. 156
10. $x = 5,\ y = 8$
11. $x = -\dfrac{1}{3},\ y = \dfrac{4}{5}$
12. $x = -4,\ y = 1,\ z = 7$
13. $A + B = \begin{bmatrix} 9 & 2 & 8 \\ 13 & -9 & 1 \\ -3 & -3 & 3 \end{bmatrix}$
14. $-4B = \begin{bmatrix} 20 & -36 & 8 \\ -16 & 44 & -72 \\ -12 & 24 & -28 \end{bmatrix}$
15. $CA = \begin{bmatrix} 36 & -44 & 124 \\ 77 & -6 & -63 \end{bmatrix}$
16. D
17. E
18. $\cot\alpha = \dfrac{1}{5}$
19. $\sin\theta + \sin\theta\cot^2\theta = \dfrac{4}{3}$
20. E
21. D
22. Maximum value of $h(g(x)) = 9$
23. $\cos y = -0.39$
24. 127 caramel corn boxes,
    91 buttered microwave popcorn boxes,
    182 lightly buttered microwave popcorn boxes

CHAPTER TEST ANSWERS

Chapter 11 Test
1. True
2. True
3. $x = \dfrac{1}{3},\ y = -\dfrac{1}{2}$
4. $(-5, 32),\ (1, -4)$
5. C
6. A
7. D
8. E
9. B
10. E
11. D
12. D
13. B
14. A
15. B
16. C
17. D
18. E
19. B
20. $k = 9$
21. $\dfrac{p}{q} = 1.12$
22. $24^x = 44.6$
23. Length of major axis $= 4$
24. 8.7 miles per hour, 6.6° north of east

Chapter 12 Test
1. True
2. False
3. $a_8 = 45$
4. $r = -\dfrac{3}{4}$
5. $g_1 = 6$
6. Sum $= 10,290$
7. Sum does not exist
8. $15 + 6 + \dfrac{12}{5} + \dfrac{24}{25} + \ldots = 25$
9. 40,320 ways
10. 20 ways
11. 2,002 boards of directors
12. 210 combinations
13. $\dfrac{1}{3}$
14. $\dfrac{5}{6}$
15. 45,697,600 confirmation codes

16. $\dfrac{1}{10}$ or 0.1
17. $\dfrac{2}{15}$
18. Mean $= 584.6$; Range $= 385$
19. Median $= 590$; Mode $= 640$
20. Standard deviation $= 110.9$
21. E
22. $a_{200} = 1,001$
23. Test average $= 80$
24. $1,725

Chapter 13 Test
1. True
2. True
3. 84 combinations
4. 2,184 possibilities
5. C
6. A
7. Mean $= 16.7$; Range $= 23$
8. Standard deviation $= 7.31$; Median $= 15$
9. Slope $= 8$
10. Slope $= -12$
11. E
12. D
13. A
14. C
15. Area $= \dfrac{64}{3}$
16. Area $= 14$
17. $\lim\limits_{x \to 2}(x^2 + 6x - 5) = 11$
18. $\lim\limits_{x \to -4}\dfrac{x^2 - 16}{x + 4} = -8$
19. E
20. B
21. $\sqrt[3]{7n} = 9.9$
22. Sum $= 1,408.5$
23. Average of points $= 63.38$
24. 128 feet/sec

Chapter 14 Test
1. True
2. True
3. $\dfrac{1}{2}$ or 0.5
4. 0.125
5. E
6. D
7. C

103

8. A

9. $\lim\limits_{x \to 2}(-x^3 - 7x^2 + 9) = -27$

10. $\lim\limits_{x \to -3}\dfrac{x^2 + 3x}{x^2 - 4x - 21} = \dfrac{3}{10}$ or 0.3

11. B

12. E

13. C

14. B

15. C

16. A

17. C

18. B

19. D

20. B

21. A

22. $m = \dfrac{1}{2}$

23. $b = -4$

24. 13.86 inches